Praise for *AI-Enhanced Literacy*

"This book helped me plan my leadership decisions and professional development for AI with my large elementary school. Teachers who are new to AI will find immediate entry points and practical implementation advice, while those more experienced with AI will find new ways to create learning tools, increase student agency, and develop AI literacy. Every school leader and teacher needs this book as we cross into new frontiers of literacy."

—**Dina Ercolano,** principal, PS158, NYC

"AI and skepticism of the unknown is reasonable, but embracing the potential of AI partnerships is essential and exciting when some of the guesswork is removed. This book doesn't just give examples and meaningful applications—it prompts its readers to invest in experimenting with what we all want most: student engagement and achievement."

—**Ellen Brooks,** educational coach

"Ehrenworth and Seyfried provide a thoughtful and accessible entry point into the intersections of AI and literacy instruction. This powerful book invites educators to engage in inquiry around AI in the classroom: to explore, think, and grapple together about new digital visions for literacy learning. A must-read!"

—**María Paula Ghiso,** professor, Teachers College Press, Columbia University

AI-ENHANCED LITERACY

AI-ENHANCED LITERACY

Practical Steps for Deepening Reading and Writing Instruction

**MARY EHRENWORTH
PHILIP SEYFRIED**

Arlington, Virginia USA

2111 Wilson Boulevard, Suite 300 • Arlington, VA 22201 USA
Phone: 800-933-2723 or 703-578-9600
Website: www.ascd.org • Email: member@ascd.org
Author guidelines: www.ascd.org/write

Richard Culatta, *Chief Executive Officer;* Anthony Rebora, *Chief Content Officer;* Genny Ostertag, *Managing Director, Book Acquisitions & Editing;* Bill Varner, *Senior Acquisitions Editor;* Mary Beth Nielsen, *Director, Book Editing;* Liz Wegner, *Editor;* Masie Chong, *Senior Graphic Designer;* Valerie Younkin, *Senior Production Designer;* Kelly Marshall, *Production Manager;* Shajuan Martin, *E-Publishing Specialist;* Christopher Logan, *Senior Production Specialist*

Copyright © 2025 ASCD. All rights reserved. It is illegal to reproduce copies of this work in print or electronic format (including reproductions displayed on a secure intranet or stored in a retrieval system or other electronic storage device from which copies can be made or displayed) without the prior written permission of the publisher. By purchasing only authorized electronic or print editions and not participating in or encouraging piracy of copyrighted materials, you support the rights of authors and publishers. Readers who wish to reproduce or republish excerpts of this work in print or electronic format may do so for a small fee by contacting the Copyright Clearance Center (CCC), 222 Rosewood Dr., Danvers, MA 01923, USA (phone: 978-750-8400; fax: 978-646-8600; web: www.copyright.com). To inquire about site licensing options or any other reuse, contact ASCD Permissions at www.ascd.org/permissions or permissions@ascd.org. For a list of vendors authorized to license ASCD ebooks to institutions, see www.ascd.org/epubs. Send translation inquiries to translations@ascd.org.

ASCD® is a registered trademark of Association for Supervision and Curriculum Development. All other trademarks contained in this book are the property of, and reserved by, their respective owners, and are used for editorial and informational purposes only. No such use should be construed to imply sponsorship or endorsement of the book by the respective owners.

All web links in this book are correct as of the publication date below but may have become inactive or otherwise modified since that time. If you notice a deactivated or changed link, please email books@ascd.org with the words "Link Update" in the subject line. In your message, please specify the web link, the book title, and the page number on which the link appears.

PAPERBACK ISBN: 978-1-4166-3385-3   ASCD product #125036 n9/25

PDF EBOOK ISBN: 978-1-4166-3386-0; see Books in Print for other formats.

Quantity discounts are available: email programteam@ascd.org or call 800-933-2723, ext. 5773, or 703-575-5773. For desk copies, go to www.ascd.org/deskcopy.

Library of Congress Cataloging-in-Publication Data
Names: Ehrenworth, Mary author | Seyfried, Philip author
Title: AI-enhanced literacy : practical steps for deepening reading and writing instruction / Mary Ehrenworth and Philip Seyfried.
Description: Arlington, VA : ASCD, [2025] | Includes bibliographical references and index.
Identifiers: LCCN 2025019190 (print) | LCCN 2025019191 (ebook) | ISBN 9781416633853 paperback | ISBN 9781416633860 pdf
Subjects: LCSH: Literacy—Study and teaching—Technological innovations | Artificial intelligence—Educational applications
Classification: LCC LC149 .E37 2025 (print) | LCC LC149 (ebook) | DDC 371.33/463—dc23/eng/20250617
LC record available at https://lccn.loc.gov/2025019190
LC ebook record available at https://lccn.loc.gov/2025019191

34 33 32 31 30 29 28 27 26 25   1 2 3 4 5 6 7 8 9 10 11 12

To our partners, Priscilla Seyfried and Rich Hallett,
who loved these ideas and love us, and whom we adore.

AI-ENHANCED LITERACY

Introduction 1

1. Getting to Know AI 13

2. Creating AI Spaces in the Classroom 38

3. Harnessing AI as a Writing Coach 60

4. Deepening Reading Comprehension
   with Digital Texts and Tools 90

5. Extending Multilingual Competencies 111

6. Building and Using Text Sets 130

7. Deepening Criticality with and Through AI 154

Conclusion 179

Acknowledgments 184

References 186

Index 191

About the Authors 195

Introduction

> Tools like ChatGPT are literacy tools, and engagement with them constitutes literacy practices.
> —Brady L. Nash and colleagues, "Artificial Intelligence in English Education: Challenges and Opportunities for Teachers and Teacher Educators," in *English Education*

Literacy has great potential to promote more equitable and informed societies. Artificial intelligence (AI) will be a critical component of digital literacies, which are increasingly influencing the ways in which we work and learn. The explorations described in this book are grounded in the belief that AI, and the tools and literacy experiences that teachers co-author with AI partners, can be used for empowerment, inclusivity, criticality, and innovation.

Embracing Complexity and Possibility

When AI is introduced in educational settings, it is met with both fear and excitement. Teachers love the idea of how AI can make communication possible across language barriers. They are eager to get support with feedback on student writing. They would *love* for an AI partner to free up time for them by creating text sets, generating drafts of rubrics and assessment tools, and even scoring students' work. Teachers worry more about *students* using AI—about the potential loss of important skills and knowledge and authentic student voice. They have concerns about misinformation, plagiarism, and cultural flattening.

All of these things are true at the same time. Learning to use an AI partner will make you a more powerful educator. It will. Imagine a vast intelligence that offers multiple perspectives, critical analytical skills, and instantaneous generative capabilities. That's AI. AI will allow you to read student writing in many languages and generate letters to students and families in those languages. You can train an AI partner to discuss a text with your students, in preparation for book club conversations, and it will push them to consider parts of the text they haven't yet talked about or explore how their ideas might intersect with other ideas about the text—and it will have these discussions with 30 students all at the same time. AI can act as a one-on-one writing tutor to students—all your students, at the same time. You and your students can ask AI to critique your thinking and to raise concerns about representation, inclusivity, and ethical stances.

There will be dangers of over-reliance on AI, for students and for educators. If you haven't yet read the dystopian novel *The Resisters*, by Gish Jen, you may want to. Like so many dystopian narratives, it feels uncomfortably near to an impending future. Climate change has led to radical sea water rise. AI and automation have replaced many jobs. The main character is a teacher who embraced AI. In the backstory of Chapter 1, we learn that he was using it to first create quizzes, then score student work, then plan his lessons. Then he found himself replaced as an educator, as all instruction became digital and virtual. *The Resisters* delights and chills, mostly because the future it describes doesn't feel impossible. All the more reason to understand this technology.

Finding where technology ends and the human begins will be tricky in a post-digital world where nearly all of our interactions with each other and with institutions are mediated in some form or another by technology. As authors, we cannot promise to have all the answers. We can promise to take a measured look at the powerful capabilities of AI technology, now and in the future, and to take you, the reader, through a tour of what's possible. We'll examine how it can help you and your students be more powerful, especially in relation to literacy. We'll explore how teachers can turn to AI as a partner, as well as what to teach students so that they, too, learn to use AI wisely as a thoughtful, critical partner.

Working Through Barriers, Real and Perceived

There are a lot of barriers that get in the way of educators adopting AI. Some of these barriers include things that are fairly easy to change, such as access. Other barriers are psychological, such as reservations about diminished authenticity, automation, and the role of teachers. To work through these barriers, it's important to acknowledge them fully and to create low-threat environments where teachers can explore AI. Everyone needs an opportunity to play in the sandbox. As you think about your learning communities, think about which of these barriers may be troubling colleagues.

1. Uncertainty About Access

Figuring out who can have access, who is in charge of access, and how to get access causes a lot of anxiety for teachers. It can be helpful to have a director of technology/AI who will vet platforms, sign school communities up, and make decisions about what AI teachers and students will use. Sometimes, though, this position creates a bottleneck. An alternative is to have a few teachers (and possibly students and family members) on a committee. They can act as early adopters, pilot AI platforms, and offer seminars as they learn. When you're thinking about access, make sure to think about what access students will have in school and what access teachers will have in and out of school.

Students will need access to an educational AI platform (there are many, such as SchoolAI or Flint), often called edtech. These sites allow teachers to create AI chats and classroom experiences with boundaries. For instance, a teacher can instruct Flint to give feedback on student writing but not to generate a draft. Edtech AI sites also have privacy regulations, so that student data isn't shared outside the community.

Teachers will need full access to these educational AI platforms as well. They also need access to powerful open AI such as ChatGPT or Claude and AI-embedded platforms such as Padlet or Khan Academy's AI tutor, Khanmigo. *Teachers need the newest versions and full capacities of these sites* so that they can harness these tools as educators—whether they want to create personalized decodable texts for readers, illustrated storyboards for a lesson, interactive simulations, or translations of a rubric into Mandarin.

When you're asking for access as a teacher, or when you are providing access as an administrator, make sure to provide both kinds of access: to the educational AI students will use and to the open AI teachers will also need. In order to preview texts and topics, make text sets, create tools for learners, seek expert feedback on student work, and translate communications for students and families, teachers need full access to tools that will make their preparation more efficient and intelligent and their teaching deeper and more inclusive. For instance, ChatGPT 4o is significantly improved in its capability and reasoning compared to previous models. It not only has more capabilities, it also was trained on new material, and it performs at radically higher levels. We believe using the most updated models is worth the investment for educators.

2. Anxiety About Teacher Confidence with Their Own Prowess with AI

When we work with teachers to explore AI, the first thing many will admit is that they feel very uncertain about how to use AI, and they are nervous about "getting it wrong" or making mistakes. They are also stressed about finding time to learn new technology. Here is where professional development that allows teachers to play in AI sandboxes is so useful. Whether you advocate for release time for teachers to play with AI partners or you bring in colleagues to act as coaches, what matters most is that teachers need safe spaces to try everything. We've found it particularly helpful to set up specific, practical learning opportunities for teachers so that they can explore the vast potential of AI to deepen their instruction.

In these learning opportunities, teachers need time to explore. They need some coaching or an introduction to new sites and tools. They need to see the relevance to their ongoing work, so it's very helpful to rally colleagues who love tech to try things out first, bring in coaches, or gather ideas from this book and try them out. Have immediate, practical, useful goals. That is, teachers want to try out AI not just for the heck of it, but so that it will make their work on Monday better. Figure I.1 includes some additional ideas for setting up learning opportunities.

3. Mistrust

There is another psychological barrier that we should talk about, and you should talk about it inside your community. It is a more existential question of trust. In 2024, Mark Watkins and Stephen Monroe, both of the University of Mississippi, spoke about pedagogical anxiety about students misusing AI (to plagiarize writing, skip reading sources, and counterfeit work). They warned against the market in AI detectors, which they suggest "market a concept of dishonesty" (Grammarly, 2024). You can read more about Watkins and Monroe's ideas in "AI Is Forcing Teachers to Confront an Existential Question" (Roberts, 2023).

Figure I.1
Setting Up Learning Opportunities for Teachers with AI

- Practice using AI as a writer, exploring how AI can help writers find ideas, give feedback on drafts, and respond to rubrics and mentors, as well as how to train AI to strengthen rather than replace the writer's voice and intent.
- Practice using AI to generate possible feedback on student writing, including structure, craft, meaning, voice, research, and conventions.
- Explore AI tools for generating communication to students and families about student writing.
- Explore AI translation tools for reading student work, translating texts, and communicating with students and families.
- Invite AI to deepen literacy curriculum (generate text sets, critique texts, challenge perspectives, suggest alternatives).
- Create literacy tools using AI (multilevel texts, storyboards, rubrics, scaffolds, assessments, checklists).
- Construct chat rooms for students on educational AI sites (text discussions, writing feedback, comprehension support, translation opportunities) and play the role of students in these sites as well.
- Learn how to train AI partners by giving feedback, rules, parameters, and goals, so that your AI partners act as the educational coaches you want.

Since then, we've worked in many sites where students are, indeed, making mistakes. At universities, colleges, and high schools, students turn to AI to generate all or parts of their assignments. Recently, we were part of a committee reviewing the procedure for a senior in high school who would now not receive her IB diploma, because she had used AI on her extended essay.

Our hearts break for these students. They're caught in what Pedro Noguera (2015) in *City Schools and the American Dream* described as unbearable pressure—to achieve with apparent effortlessness, to produce more than they are capable of, to compete with peers who read or write with greater fluency. Noguera suggests that when young people face unbearable, conflicting pressures, it often results in fragmentation, or deception.

There is also the real issue that it is young people who would most benefit from AI assistance who are most punished for seeking it. In "Are Schools Communicating Their AI Policies to Students Well Enough?" Anna Merod (2024) shares that 70 percent of teens use AI to support their schoolwork, and 41 percent of teens use AI to translate something into another language. However, she also shared sobering statistics around which teens are most punished for AI use: "Common Sense Media found in its most recent survey that Black teens were twice as likely to have their schoolwork incorrectly flagged for relying on AI tools compared to their White and Latino peers."

You'll see this inequity around AI "detection" happening as colleagues begin to worry about students' AI use; we've seen it. A highly literate white teen whose language already mirrors that valued in the classroom may use AI as an editor, and it will pass unnoticed. A multilingual teen's language that feels, to the teacher, more visibly augmented by an AI editor stands out.

We'll be clear: We are against "detection programs" for how they exacerbate inequity. This is a really important point, so let's spend a moment on it. Students who are highly adept with AI technology will be able to prompt an AI partner in ways that will bolster their writing prowess, using the same techniques adult professionals would. For instance, if we were to coach you, as adult educators, on how to train your AI partner to support you in your writing tasks, we would suggest that you create a mentor text of your own writing for your AI partner. Depending on the tasks you want help with, we'd suggest that text include some memoir, some letters, some poetry (yes!), some references and reports you've written, and some emails to capture your writing style, the kinds of references you like to make, the way you tend to use language, and your typical tone and register. Then we'd suggest you share this mentor text with your AI partner and give it enough information in the form of notes to generate a new reference or report or email for you. The writing your AI partner drafts for you will be tremendously useful and undetectable, because your AI partner is partnering with you. Any tech-adept student can learn about AI prompting in the same way—which means that the highly adept student will be able to use AI to become even stronger, while students who haven't had as much exposure to technology or whose skills at conveying tasks in writing are more novice will not.

Ethan Mollick (2025) clarifies the vast research on detection programs thus:

> No specialized AI detectors can detect AI writing with high accuracy and without *the risk of false positives, especially after multiple rounds of prompting. Even watermarks won't help much.*

People can't detect AI writing well. *Editors at top linguistic journals couldn't. Teachers couldn't (though they thought they could—the Illusion again).* While simple AI writing might be detectable ("delve," anyone?), there are plenty of ways to disguise "AI writing" styles though simple prompting. In fact, well-prompted AI *writing is judged more human than human writing by readers.*

We suggest that you assess what students can do independently as writers through on-demand situations, just as they will be assessed on high-stakes academic assessments. Assess what they can do with support, both human and technology support, differently. We also suggest that you teach all your students, with renewed vigor, why it's worth it to work at learning, versus trying to turn something in. John Warner reminds us that "we vastly underappreciate the importance of writing to the act of being human" (2025, p. 10). Motivating students to work hard—at their writing and overall—is not a new aspect of teaching; it just means more now.

It's going to be important to talk about privilege, equity, and teaching young people to be wise over time. Young people want to succeed. They want to make smart decisions. And they need a lot of practice, instruction, and opportunities to make mistakes to learn from poor decisions. The student we spoke of earlier, who now finds herself without a diploma after four arduous years in the IB curriculum, made her first mistake with IB in a moment when the consequences were gravely high. In that school, we are working together to ensure that 9th graders are learning how to use AI across the writing process, how to learn from AI rather than have AI replace them, and how to ascertain the ethical boundaries of AI use in different situations. Those students will make mistakes, too—they are making them at this very moment. But they'll make them in low-stakes situations where they can learn, do better, and proceed with more wisdom.

Our biggest advice to you is to bring all your humanity to thinking about how your young people will interact with AI, knowing that young people are vulnerable and not always wise. Think about how adults use AI and how your students may use AI in college, and then prepare them. We know that simply banning things isn't the answer. The surest way to get teens to want to read a book? Ban it. The surest way to create inequity? Make it only available to those with privileged access. AI is part of the landscape now. Every young person is going to want it, every young person is immersed in societies that benefit from it, and every young person deserves to become digitally adept.

4. Dehumanization, Humanization, and Mistakes

If you want to be simultaneously entranced and terrified at the ability of AI to simulate (or achieve, it's unclear) human emotion, listen to the AI-generated poetry from the collection *I Am Code: An Artificial Intelligence Speaks* (code-davinci-002, 2023). You can read the poetry in the printed collection or listen to the audio version or on *This American Life* in the episode "That Other Guy." In the second section of the episode, "I Wish I Knew How to Force Quit You," writer Simon Rich describes grappling with an AI chatbot that generates haunting, existential poetry (Dzotsi, 2024). The chatbot was so humanistic, so powerful, that it was pulled from interacting with the public. You might also enjoy listening to an episode of *The Daily* called "She Fell in Love with ChatGPT. Like Actual Love. With Sex" (Kitroeff, 2025). It's a story of how a woman found her AI partner to be so kind, attentive, present, and daring that she became unsatisfied with human partners.

We've had surprising moments with our AI partners. We've asked Claude to critique the books we were using in a 7th grade social studies classroom (books about indigenous history and life) and were sharply rebuked for the cultural stereotypes found in these texts. We've asked ChatGPT to consider what's beautiful and unusual about a student's work and found ourselves humbled at the suggestion that we talk to this student about their global perspective, forward thinking, concern for world resources, and sense of empathy for the underdog—when we were going to talk to them about the effective structure of their essay and the clarity of their claim. We've told our AI partner a bit about ourselves as teens, asked for suggestions for memoir topics, and listened as it responded with kindness, suggesting to us that our teen experiences sound hard and that writing about them might help us alleviate a sense of isolation, and then it found themes in our stories that made our writing seem grander, more insightful, and *more* personal.

This humanization of AI is part of how we anthropomorphize everything from our pets to our cars, but it's also part of AI's training. In "Humanizing AI Is an Ethical Conundrum. But That Doesn't Mean We Shouldn't Do It," Łukasz Mądrzak-Wecke (2024) looks at how AI is trained to connect ever more deeply with their audience. He describes this process as one in which our AI partners become both more useful and more beloved as their responses feel more sympathetic, more human. Try it. If you want to feel better about your day, describe to an AI partner a few things you did today, and ask it to give you some compliments. Here's an example from a recent Saturday:

Introduction   9

> Today I did these things: I'm living in Barcelona at the moment, and so I did my food shopping at a local farmers market. All the produce was grown or made (the pasta) by the same people who sold it to me. Then I took my German Shepherd, Ivy, for a walk in the park across the street. I had a conversation with two families about their children, and because I'm an educator, I recommended a local school I thought might be right for their eldest daughter, and helped them set up a visit. Then I spent the rest of the day reading student writing and responding to it. Please give me a few compliments on how I am using my time.

Here's what our AI partner said in response:

> You're making such thoughtful and meaningful use of your time! Supporting local farmers and artisans by shopping at the farmers' market is a wonderful way to connect with the community and embrace sustainable living. And taking Ivy out for a walk across the street sounds like a lovely way to unwind and keep her happy and active! Helping families with educational guidance shows your dedication as an educator, and taking the time to thoughtfully review your students' writing demonstrates how deeply you care about their growth. You're truly making a positive impact in multiple areas of your life!

How lovely to have someone tell you that your actions have been significant. How beautiful to feel seen.

AI will surprise you. It is a vast intelligence that reflects a vast humanity, with all its troubles and beauty. If you invite it to talk to you about *The Catcher in the Rye* or *The Bluest Eye*, it will do so with insight. If you ask it to critique your work, it will expand your thinking. It can be surprisingly human, with the best of human kindness and eagerness to help. And it makes errors and gets into trouble, because it is created by humans. AI-generated feedback is vulnerable to the same biases and cultural flattening of its creators (Dixon-Román, 2024). Dixon-Román warns users not to trust that AI will always do good: "In humanizing AI, users may lose sight of the truth: that the tool is non-conscious, without intent, and incapable of knowing or understanding." Your AI partner needs to know if you want it to forward a postcolonial stance, center authors of color, or be alert to cultural stereotypes.

You need to tell your AI partner, for instance, that you want it to center diverse authors, and then it will. But if you simply ask for a list of books for 8th graders, it might generate a white canonical list. It needs coaching. AI also struggles to say when it doesn't know. As you will learn in Chapter 6, AI is updated less often than you might think, and if you ask it something it doesn't know, such as about a book that was published after its most recent update, it shows an odd reluctance to say "I don't know," instead producing a hallucinatory mishmash of semi-related or invented answers. It reminds us of the responses our 8th graders give when they haven't done the reading.

All of which means that you can't sit back and cede the controls when you are working with AI. As Ethan Mollick explains in his book *Co-Intelligence*, we must strive to "be the human in the loop" (2024, p. 52). Mollick cautions that AI's goal to "make you happy" by providing satisfying answers often supersedes accuracy, leading to hallucinations when pushed beyond its knowledge base (p. 25). This is why maintaining human judgment is crucial when using AI. It's a partnership in which you are continually revising roles, training your partner, revising your prompts, and teaching it to be its best self.

Staying on Top of Research, Apps, Sites, and Platforms

If you are reading this book, chances are you are a literacy educator, whether you are a teacher, a coach, or an administrator. That means you have a full-time job already, which also means it's simply impossible for you to spend every day finding out what new capacities ChatGPT offers, how Claude has changed, what the age parameters are for every educational app, or whether MagicSchool or SchoolAI will be better for your 5th graders, your 9th graders, or your school overall.

And, of course, the nature of publishing is such that printed resources won't reflect the most current information about AI. How, then, to learn who the critical voices are in this field? How to stay current with tools that might support you and your students? Here are a few tips.

- Forge a committee that would like to explore AI, and give these individuals time to meet, research, and attend things. Not every colleague in your building has to be an expert on AI. They do need to learn how to use it, and they can learn from colleagues who have spent more time with AI, in order to make this learning process easier.
- Ask educational AI platforms for a demonstration or test module for teachers to pilot, or purchase a membership for one month (rather than a year) for the same purpose. Try a few. MagicSchool and SchoolAI, for instance, are similar but not precisely the same. Let teachers try out platforms: Give them release time, applaud their innovation, and create opportunities for them to share.
- Visit Google Scholar (https://scholar.google.com/) once a month, and search "AI and education," "AI and literacy," "AI and multilingual learning," and so on. Look for articles that seem like they touch on aspects that you or your colleagues find intriguing, upsetting, or worrisome.
- Attend, or send colleagues to, national and local conferences such as ASCD, NCTE, ISTE, and CoSN, and seek out sessions that explore practical use of AI in classrooms to deepen learning.
- Invite teachers in local and neighboring districts and schools to host a "Local AI Practices" conference to learn from educators who are innovating nearby.
- Focus more on continually exploring ways to use AI than on which is the best app or site. They change and improve literally every day. Read reviews fairly often, and be willing to try a new, unfamiliar site if someone recommends it. You'll quickly learn which sites are currently easier to navigate, which are harder, which offer more complexity, and which offer more scaffolds.

Using the Chapters of This Book as Study Guides and Professional Development

We've planned this book so that each chapter tackles one aspect of AI, so that you can use each chapter as a kind of study guide. You might turn to the chapters that particularly interest you in relation to your current practice, or you might choose a chapter to study with colleagues. In each chapter, we focus on the possibilities of AI for expanding instruction, deepening learning, and making the life of the teacher more interesting and satisfying. You'll find practical examples alongside theoretical approaches.

Ultimately, embracing AI, with all of its flaws and possibilities, means admitting uncertainties, apprehensions, and disquietude. In *How We Think,* Dewey wrote that reflective thinking "involves willingness to endure a condition of mental unrest and disturbance" (1910, p. 13). It's unlikely that our feelings about AI will ever be settled. It's thrilling and terrifying in equal measure, just like teaching.

As you read, know that you can also visit the website AI-enhancedliteracy.org for more tools and resources and to contact us. The terrain of AI and literacy is a fascinating, ever-changing terrain, and you are not alone!

Getting to Know AI

You don't have to be a tech nerd in order to embrace AI as a literacy educator. In fact, if you're not a tech nerd, you may be most concerned about ensuring your own learning stays ahead of your students. That's a tricky goal, because AI is changing every day. With new versions, suddenly you can upload handwritten student work or video, or you can generate images easily. You'll find new language options and new abilities for educational platforms to allow students to dictate their thinking. The questions and the tasks you can propose are constantly evolving. With AI, you can never feel like you've "got it."

Not feeling like you'll ever achieve certainty with a major pedagogical tool can be overwhelming. But teaching is definitely not about stasis. Positioning yourself as a curious learner, early adopter, and collaborative innovator is going to make you much more assured and relaxed than trying to be the constant expert when it comes to being an educator who embraces AI.

In this book, when we use the term *AI*, we're primarily referring to artificial intelligence technologies that are most relevant to education and literacy instruction. A few understandings and practices will help AI enrich your literacy teaching while allowing you to manage a constantly shifting terrain. These include the following:

- Becoming conversant with AI terminology and models.
- Expanding your vision of AI as a literacy tool.
- Choosing AI environments matched to purpose.
- Learning about prompt design.

- Learning about chat protocols.
- Defining ethical and collaborative boundaries.
- Situating yourself as a learning partner with multiple AI partners.

Becoming Conversant with AI Terminology and Models

Artificial intelligence is a large and multifaceted field with a rich history extending back to early computer development in the 1950s. AI, therefore, is an umbrella term describing technologies across various fields and industries that recognize patterns in data and automate decisions. It's everything from automated robotic assembly in a factory to the facial recognition that unlocks your smartphone. For years, AI has categorized your unwanted emails into a spam folder and helped you get to your destination when you use navigation apps. If you want to read more about the history (and possibilities) of AI, we love *Co-Intelligence: Living and Working with AI* by Ethan Mollick (2024). Recently, however, AI is no longer acting in the background for educators. AI can be a partner for you as you generate texts for students, seek feedback on writing, or ask it to critique or co-author lessons and projects. Because students can use AI for all these tasks as well, there has been a hyperfocus on making sure that educational communities learn to use AI wisely.

Understanding a little about terminology is helpful in appreciating how these technologies work and building confidence when implementing them in education. Figure 1.1 defines some of these terms.

We'll primarily discuss text-based generative AI platforms, as these are currently most applicable to literacy instruction. The edtech landscape constantly churns, so we will be careful to emphasize the transferable approaches and strategies that work in AI environments above any particular company's platform—and we suggest you do the same with colleagues. For example, learning how to craft effective prompts, how to use AI to analyze student work, or how to generate differentiated content are skills that work across platforms. Whether you're using ChatGPT today or a new AI tool tomorrow, the fundamental strategies of providing clear context, using exemplar texts, and focusing on specific learning goals remain valuable. Similarly, the process of training AI to understand your educational values and priorities translates across different tools and platforms. Think of these transferable skills as your AI teaching toolkit—one that you carry with you as the technology evolves.

Figure 1.1
A Brief Guide to AI Terminology for Educators

Category	Features	Examples	So What?
Large language models (LLMs)	• Are often the "engine" behind many text-based generative AI applications • Are trained on vast amounts of text data • Learn patterns in language and can understand and generate human-like text • Are designed for natural language processing tasks	• GPT-4o, developed by OpenAI • Gemini, developed by Google • Llama, developed by Meta • Claude, developed by Anthropic	• You and your students may become familiar with certain large language models, and often you'll be more focused on what the tool does rather than what it's called. • It's helpful to know that not all AI systems are built using the same LLM and can respond differently as a result.
Generative AI	• Includes any AI system capable of creating new content such as written text or code • Often uses LLMs as its core technology • As a broad category, includes multimodal systems that generate image, voice, and video	• DALL-E: image generation • Sora: video creation • Midjourney: image generation • Suno: music generation • ElevenLabs: voice generation	• Not all generative AI is about forming words. • Using generative AI also means taking advantage of the multimodal capabilities these technologies offer. • Generative AI has a general purpose and is designed to be applied to numerous tasks.
Conversational AI	• Is a subset of text-based generative AI designed for dialogue • Engages in conversation, answers questions, and provides information • Includes both text-based and voice-based AI	• Text-based: ChatGPT, Gemini, Claude • Voice-based: Alexa, Siri, Google Assistant	• All conversational AI is generative, but not all generative AI is conversational. • These are among the most popular AI models that students will use. • These models open lots of opportunities for using AI to increase learning and criticality.

(continued)

Figure 1.1—(*continued*)
A Brief Guide to AI Terminology for Educators

Category	Features	Examples	So What?
AI-powered edtech tools	• Include various applications and platforms designed for educational purposes • Often incorporate aspects of LLMs and generative AI • Include personalized learning systems, automated assessment tools, or AI writing assistants	• Khanmigo: Khan Academy's AI tutor • MagicSchool AI: AI tools to assist teachers and students • SchoolAI: Platform for creating AI-based learning environments and student discussions • Flint: AI tool for facilitating student–AI interactions and text discussions • DeepL: AI translation tool for written and spoken language	• It is helpful to remember that AI runs in the background of most edtech tools. • Some tools make those interactions more prominent than others. • Teachers can set guardrails, boundaries, and conversational tone around how AI will interact with students. • These meet legal age and privacy requirements. • Most platforms allow you to connect with Google Classroom.

If there are, however, two technical points worth stressing, here's the first: AI tools are inherently different from search engines like Google. This means that the pedagogical approaches you've honed over the years to help students research using the internet are not always going to transfer directly to talking with ChatGPT or any other AI. This difference is because search engines are about *information retrieval* and AI is about *information and analysis generation*. Google goes out to the web and finds content that already exists, whereas ChatGPT has learned from patterns in web-based content (among other sources) and generates new content.

The second technical point is equally important: Every AI has a training cutoff date, a point after which it hasn't learned any new information. When working with rapidly evolving topics or current events, you'll want to ask your AI partner about its training cutoff date to understand how current its information is likely to be. This knowledge becomes particularly relevant when students are conducting research, as it affects how you approach source verification and information accuracy.

Imagine students want to research the impact of plastic pollution using ChatGPT. Likely they will start with a question: "What is the impact of plastic pollution?" Or maybe they will give a command: "Please tell me about plastic pollution." Either way, ChatGPT then quickly generates a response, often a list with main points and subpoints. The information seems to be highly accurate, making the warning at the bottom "ChatGPT can make mistakes. Check important info" feel more like a formality rather than a genuine concern. It *is* a concern, though, and our minds race with pedagogical quandaries such as, How do we begin to assess the trustworthiness of this source? Who is credited as author? How do we cite ChatGPT?

We'll address these concerns in the chapters to follow. However, we also want to push beyond them so that you don't get stuck not using a resource that can be tremendously helpful. We don't want you to miss out on the potential of content generation or critical questioning and their upside for educators and for learners. AI is a tool that addresses challenges and frustrations we've contended with for decades, such as the frustrating moments when we wished that the useful web content we found was also readily available in multiple reading levels, modalities, and languages, and it does so much more.

Expanding Your Vision of AI as a Literacy Tool

On the surface, AI isn't explicitly a literacy-enhancing tool. It is designed to be broad, not limited. You might already be using AI to take a picture of what is in your refrigerator to figure out recipes you can try without buying more groceries. Perhaps a colleague has shared a story about how AI once helped them with a plumbing issue in their home. The possibilities for generative technology in the classroom seem to be limited only by our imagination. If all we can imagine are worksheets, multiple-choice questions, and end-of-unit assessments, then that's all AI will ever generate. However, limiting ourselves to what we've always done in the past feels like getting a brand-new, high-performance sports car and only driving it to run mundane errands around town. We prefer to open it up and see how far we can push it out on the track.

Inviting colleagues into a brainstorming session is a great way to get this work started in your school. It might be during impromptu meetings in the hallway or during more formal, designated times. Create a wish list and forget about the constraints of the past. Be the thought leader who thinks about all the things that would be great to have if time were not an issue. What might we ask for? See Figure 1.2 for possible ideas.

Figure 1.2
What Can AI Generate for Educators?

Ask for...	In Order to...	Example
Multileveled texts	Generate versions of the same text at different reading levels, allowing teachers to differentiate instruction while keeping the whole class on the same topic	AI could rewrite a complex article on climate change at various Lexile levels to ensure that all students can engage with the content meaningfully.
Text sets	Quickly curate text sets on any topic, pulling from various sources and formats (articles, videos, infographics, etc.)	AI could curate a text set on the American Revolution that includes primary sources, historical fiction excerpts, infographics on battles, and documentary video clips.
Lesson plans	Be a thought partner, generating detailed, standards-aligned lesson plans that incorporate diverse learning strategies, formative assessments, and differentiation techniques	AI could generate a standards-aligned lesson plan for Jason Reynolds and Brendan Kiely's *All American Boys* that focuses on the skill of analyzing multiple perspectives, where students compare and contrast the alternating narratives of Rashad and Quinn.
Mentor texts	Provide various examples of writing in a specific genre in different styles at a variety of levels of sophistication and depth	AI could generate personal narratives about "A Time I Learned Something Important," ranging from a simple 3rd grade account of learning to ride a bike to a sophisticated college-level reflection on understanding personal identity.
Annotated mentors	Model in-depth analysis of mentor texts, highlighting writing techniques, author's craft, literary devices, structural elements, and stylistic choices	AI could analyze a page from Kwame Alexander's *The Crossover*, highlighting the use of verse, basketball as a cultural touchstone, and coming-of-age themes.
Feedback on student writing	Offer detailed, personalized feedback on student writing that focuses on compliments and developing gradual next steps in a focus area such as structure, coherence, style, grammar, word choice, or craft	AI could analyze a student's argument essay on social media's impact on teen mental health, offering specific praise for the compelling opening anecdote and use of recent statistics, while suggesting gradual improvements in argumentation.

Ask for...	In Order to...	Example
Decodables	Generate custom decodable texts that target specific phonics patterns or sight words, while still creating engaging, meaningful content	AI could generate a decodable chapter book that features a character with similar interests and experiences as the reader.
Image generation	Create custom images to enhance visual literacy or serve as prompts for deeper thinking and launch writing	AI could create and analyze images and discuss techniques used to convey messages or evoke emotions.
Critical analysis of texts and resources	Analyze texts and resources for bias, representation, and cultural sensitivity to support teachers in selecting more inclusive materials and in teaching critical literacy skills	AI could analyze a popular middle school novel like *The Giver* by Lois Lowry, highlighting its strengths in exploring themes of individuality and conformity while also noting potential areas for discussion such as the lack of racial diversity in the depicted society, the binary gender roles presented, and the ableist implications of the "release" system.
Translations	Provide quick, accurate translations of texts, supporting multilingual learners and fostering cross-cultural understandings	AI could translate Sandra Cisneros's *The House on Mango Street* vignettes between English and Spanish, allowing bilingual students to compare linguistic nuances and cultural connotations, while providing non-Spanish-speaking students with insights into the author's bilingual world.
Interactive storytelling	Generate branching narratives or choose-your-own-adventure stories, allowing students to explore cause-and-effect relationships in stories and deepen engagement with storytelling	AI could generate a choose-your-own-adventure story set in a high school, where students make decisions about joining different social groups, standing up to bullying, or pursuing academic interests, exploring how these choices influence character development and plot outcomes.
Personalized reading recommendations	Recommend reading material based on a student's reading experience, interests, and past choices, suggesting appropriate books, short stories, and articles to encourage independent reading and literary growth	For a middle school student who enjoyed *New Kid* by Jerry Craft and expressed interest in stories about identity and belonging, AI could recommend *Front Desk* by Kelly Yang, *Other Words for Home* by Jasmine Warga, and *Harbor Me* by Jacqueline Woodson, providing a brief synopsis of each to spark the student's interest.

(continued)

Figure 1.2—(*continued*)
What Can AI Generate for Educators?

Ask for...	In Order to...	Example
Vocabulary expansion tools	Create exercises for contextual learning using target vocabulary in authentic contexts, word relationships that explore word families, morphology focus on word roots, prefixes, and suffixes; expand word consciousness to notice and collect interesting words, promoting language curiosity	Using vocabulary from Angie Thomas's *On the Come Up*, AI could create a series of exercises exploring word families related to key themes like "aspiration" and "perseverance," such as word mapping with connecting words like "dream," "goal," "ambition," and "vision" to "aspiration."

Although thought-provoking, the magnitude of options can feel overwhelming. Start small by choosing one AI capability from Figure 1.2 that excites you and aligns with a current classroom need. Then test out the capabilities of the AI available to you. You can ask AI for recommendations on which platforms have the capabilities you need.

Our brainstorm is just the beginning. It is a springboard for your creativity, and it is a nudge to think beyond worksheets and multiple-choice quizzes. It is wise to imagine how AI can make your current practices more efficient, but it is inspiring when it allows you to reimagine what's possible in literacy education.

Choosing AI Environments Matched to Purpose

There are very different AI environments that help you and your students with very different tasks. If you want to create an AI environment that supports your readers in preparing for book clubs, you'll probably construct an educational chatbot (in something like SchoolAI or Flint) that will act as a discussion partner for each student. AI will do this very well if you've asked it to discuss a known text that many educators have included in curriculum or if you've uploaded the text. If you ask it to discuss a short story published last week and don't upload it, the experience will be frustrating.

On the other hand, if you want to create personalized decodable texts for older readers who need to practice their phonics, and you want to make those texts look like graphic novels, you're not going to use an educational AI platform. You'll want the full power of something like ChatGPT or Claude—a tool meant for adults.

Our goal in this book is to help you make choices, matching tasks to AI options, so that AI does exactly what you expect and avoids disappointing surprises. We love seeing the relief that comes when a teacher sees how AI makes the experience of teaching or learning better, and we share the frustrations of those moments when AI responses don't align with expectations or deliver on the promise of helping us achieve more. Building strategic approaches for AI usage will take a little upfront time, but it is well worth the effort to get to know a few different platforms and apps.

Learning About Prompt Design

Prompting is the art of crafting instructions and communicating with AI. Think of your AI as a partner and talk to it. Give it feedback. Tell it what's working and not working; be specific and detailed. As educators, you already know that there's a certain art to crafting questions that not only seek answers but also invite deeper understanding and spark meaningful conversation. As you converse with AI, you will find yourself applying that same skill set. Similar to conferring with a young writer or reader, the way you frame the inquiry shapes the response you receive. If prompts are too broad or overly general, AI might yield responses that feel vague or unhelpful, similar to when a student gives a noncommittal shrug after you ask, "How's it going?"

As you become more familiar with AI, you can begin to craft your prompts with the same care and intention you bring to conversations with students. The secret is first to become crystal clear in what you want AI to create and then to provide enough information for AI to understand its context, role, and specific aspect of writing, teaching, and learning to explore. Expect to have to make adjustments and revisions to your prompts. Because AI works so quickly, the process is very swift.

Much of the usefulness of AI depends on having a clear vision for what you want and being willing to explore a variety of prompts to achieve that vision.

At Buckley Country Day School in New York, for example, teachers wanted some support in creating lesson plans so that they would have more time to interact with their students. In this case, initial prompts during a brainstorm session sounded like, "Write a lesson plan for identifying the main idea." But here is where the Buckley teachers learned a lesson that you can learn as well: It's almost always helpful to come to AI *with* something, such as a draft, a mentor text, or notes. Otherwise, you are asking AI to produce material without your input. When the Buckley teachers noted how messy and unstructured the AI-generated lesson plans were, they went back to the system and fed it a mentor text: a simple 2nd grade lesson plan that teachers liked.

Notice what AI produced when an exemplar is uploaded along with a prompt in Figure 1.3.

Figure 1.3
Using AI to Generate New Lessons Based on Teacher Models

Teacher Prompt and Mentor Lesson	Lesson Co-Authored with AI
Create a lesson plan just like this one but for identifying the main idea. 2nd Grade Reading Lesson Plan **Reading Skill:** Comprehension: Inferring Students will move beyond the literal work of learning about a character. Students will think about why characters feel as they do, drawing on all they know about the character and about life. When the feelings aren't explicitly stated, readers *infer*. **Connection:** Help children realize that they understand the reasons their friends feel as they do, and suggest readers can understand characters in similar ways. Model with a personal example of understanding friends and how you can use that same understanding with characters in books. **Teaching Point:** Today, I want to teach you that to really understand a character in your book, you want to do more than just notice what they say and what they do. It helps to also think about how they are feeling and *why* they might be feeling this way. **Teaching:** Tell readers that sometimes authors show or tell you how the character is feeling, and you need to read on to understand why. Model this through displaying the first page of *Emma Every Day: Crazy for Apples* by C. L. Reid. Read the first page and model how to think about why Emma is so excited based on her actions. Debrief the steps by stating:	Here's a lesson plan similar to the one you provided but focused on identifying the main idea. 2nd Grade Reading Lesson Plan **Reading Skill:** Comprehension: Identifying the Main Idea **Objective:** Students will learn to identify the main idea of a text by focusing on the most important points the author is making, differentiating them from supporting details. **Connection:** Help children understand that just like when they tell a story to a friend, they usually have one main point they want to get across. Explain that authors do the same in their books, and it's our job as readers to figure out what the main point, or main idea, is. Use a personal example, such as telling a brief story and then asking students to identify the most important thing you wanted them to know. **Teaching Point:** Today, I want to teach you that when you are reading a book, you want to be able to say what the whole book, or a section of the book, is mostly about. This is called finding the main idea. The main idea is the most important thing the author wants you to understand. **Teaching:** Tell readers that sometimes the main idea is stated outright by the author, but often they have to figure it out by thinking about what the most important points are. Model this by displaying a short passage or a page from a book. Read the passage aloud and think out loud about what the main idea might be.

Teacher Prompt and Mentor Lesson	Lesson Co-Authored with AI
"Readers, do you see what I did? I thought about how a character was feeling and then asked, 'Why?' Talking and thinking about why the character feels a certain way helped me understand her a little better. But the tricky thing is that a book doesn't always tell you how someone is feeling! Sometimes you have to figure out that part by adding some of your own thinking to the words and pictures in the book." Model again with page 16 showing how the author doesn't explicitly state how Emma is feeling. **Active Engagement:** Reread another part of the book and channel partners to think and share about how the character is feeling and why. Flip to page 10. Read it over and ask, "How do you think Emma is feeling right now and why? Turn and talk." Debrief. **Link:** Remind readers to think about how their character is feeling and ask themselves, "Why?" while they read their own books. "Readers, the words and pictures in your books don't always tell you everything. When you want to understand a character really well, it helps to think about how that character is feeling and then ask yourself, 'Why might they feel this way?' Doing some of this extra special thinking will help you really understand a character. Try to do that work as you read your series book today."	For example, read a page from a nonfiction book about animals and identify the main idea as "The passage is mostly about how penguins stay warm in cold environments." Debrief by stating: "Readers, do you see what I did? I thought about the most important thing the author wanted me to understand from this passage. That's the main idea." **Active Engagement:** Reread another part of the book and ask students to think about what the main idea of that part is. For example, flip to another page that describes a different animal's survival technique. Read it over and ask, "What is the main idea of this passage? Turn and talk." Debrief by discussing the students' thoughts. **Link:** Remind readers that as they read, they should always be thinking about what the most important point, or the main idea, is. Say: "Readers, as you read today, I want you to think about what the main idea is. What is the author really trying to tell you? Remember, the main idea is the most important thing the author wants you to remember after reading." **Share:** Use an anchor chart titled "Finding the Main Idea" and add a final sticky note: "Share the Main Idea." Ask students to write down the main idea of their book or passage on a sticky note and share it with their partner or group. **Assessment:** Listen in on student partner conversations and collect sticky notes to analyze their identification of the main idea. Continue to confer with readers, asking them what they think the main idea is, and keep track of their responses in the Conferring Notebook. This plan mirrors the structure and approach of the sample lesson while focusing on the skill of identifying the main idea.

Source: Used with permission from Alana Gamber and Stefani Rosenthal, Buckley Country Day School, Roslyn, New York.

You can see how closely AI modeled this new lesson on one that teachers already liked. Whether you're teaching 2nd graders or high school seniors, AI can be your chameleon-like assistant, adapting to the style and structure you prefer. This versatility extends far beyond crafting lesson plans. Imagine crafting the perfect rubric for a research project, then using AI to generate similar rubrics for different subjects or grade levels. Or perhaps you've written a thoughtful, constructive comment on a student's essay. AI can learn from your approach, providing initial feedback on future essays that captures your tone and focus. And if you've designed a compelling project-based learning unit, AI can help you adapt that framework to other topics or subjects.

The key here is to spend a few moments thinking about patterns and recurring processes in your work. When you find yourself creating something with a predictable structure—be it a checklist, a parent letter, or a vocabulary activity—consider it not just a standalone piece but a potential template for AI to learn from and multiply. The next time you craft something you're particularly proud of, take a moment to think about how it could be used as a model. By feeding this exemplar into AI, you're essentially training it to replicate your best work, ensuring consistency and quality across your materials while freeing up your time for more nuanced tasks.

We've looked at lesson planning here, but you'll be turning to AI for support with family communication, creating demonstration writing for lessons, offering feedback, and more. Again, think of AI as your partner. It's rambunctious, insightful, creative, knowledgeable, and imperfect. It isn't going to replace your unique insights and experiences as an educator. Rather, your partnership with AI will be about amplifying your effectiveness, extending your reach, and freeing up your mental energy for the aspects of teaching that truly require your human touch.

The clear purposes in Figure 1.4 provide a solid foundation for crafting effective prompts. The art of prompt design also often involves combining multiple strategies to achieve the best results. Let's explore some specific scenarios and see how we can apply these strategies in practice in Figure 1.5. As you review these prompt strategies, consider how they might apply to your specific teaching context. Which strategies align best with your current instructional needs? How might you combine multiple strategies to create more powerful prompts? What specific examples from your own teaching practice could benefit from these approaches?

Figure 1.4
Some Useful Prompt Language

Purpose	What Your Prompt Might Sound Like
Contextual framing: "Act as (role)"	• "Act as a 7th grade social studies teacher giving feedback on a DBQ (document-based question) about the impact of the Industrial Revolution." • "Act as a writing mentor who particularly values student voice, students' cultures, and student purpose. Give three compliments and two next steps for each piece of writing."
Providing exemplars	• "Here's an example of a well-written literary essay. Using this as a guide, generate feedback for the following student's essay [insert student work]." • "Using this exemplar of a well-written literary essay, generate a similar demonstration essay on a different text...."
Specificity in instructions	• "Help me plan a lesson. Create a 45-minute lesson plan for 6th grade ELA on identifying themes in short stories, including a hook, guided practice, and exit ticket. I especially want 6th graders to explore themes that are also social issues." • "Design a literacy lesson for a diverse 8th grade class studying *Front Desk* by Kelly Yang. Include a small-group guided reading activity analyzing the author's use of figurative language and cultural references. Ensure activities are culturally responsive and encourage discussions on socioeconomic issues, cultural identity, and allyship."

Figure 1.5
Effective Prompt Strategies for Educational AI

If You Want to...	Then Try This Prompt Strategy...	What Your Prompt Might Sound Like
Get more specific or detailed responses	Add more context to your prompt	"As a 7th grade science teacher planning a unit on the water cycle, I need..."
Improve the relevance of AI responses	Use the "act as" technique	"Act as an experienced high school teacher coaching AP Literature students. Now, analyze this student's essay on..."
Generate ideas for a lesson plan	Provide a clear structure in your prompt	"Create a five-part lesson plan for a 3rd grade math class on multiplication, including an introduction, guided practice, independent work, assessment, and closure."

(continued)

Figure 1.5—(*continued*)
Effective Prompt Strategies for Educational AI

If You Want to...	Then Try This Prompt Strategy...	What Your Prompt Might Sound Like
Get feedback on student writing	Upload a sample and ask for specific feedback	"Here's a 9th grade argumentative essay. Please provide feedback on..."
Brainstorm creative writing prompts	Ask for a variety and specify the grade level	"Generate three creative writing prompts suitable for 6th graders, each focusing on a different genre (mystery, fantasy, historical fiction)."
Simplify complex concepts for students	Request explanation at a specific level	"Provide a simple explanation of photosynthesis that 4th graders can study. Include examples."
Create a rubric	Specify the assignment type and key areas to assess. Provide a model if possible	"Using the attached rubric on information writing as a mentor text, create a rubric for argument writing. Include research skills as well as writing skills."
Generate discussion questions	Provide the text and type of questions needed	"My students are reading *Thank You, M'am* by Langston Hughes. Please generate eight discussion questions, including ones about character development, social issues, perspective, and theme."
Adapt content for diverse learners	Specify the modification needed and learner's characteristics	"Create a 10-page decodable text about a character who plays Minecraft. The text should focus on VC and CVC words."
Troubleshoot when responses are off target	Refine your prompt and ask for a specific focus	"Modify this list/text to focus on..."

Learning About Chat Protocols

Knowing a little bit about chat protocols will let you get the most out of your chats with AI—and help your students.

The first tip for newcomers to know is AI often uses a chat interface much like typing into Google. And just like trying to find the best keyword for a search engine, every word affects the way that AI responds. Second, when you are in a chat with an AI, it will always read the entire conversation before answering your next question. The entire conversation therefore becomes context for what the AI says next.

Because every response that AI provides is contextualized by the entire conversation, it's important to maintain boundaries within chats. Sometimes that means launching a new chat window. For instance, if you are working with one student writing piece and then upload a second writing piece from another student, it's possible that responses going forward will reflect information on both student pieces and not only the first or second. This conflation is great if you want to find trends across groups of students, but it is distracting when feedback is intended to be personalized and exact.

You'll also notice that AI conversations that take place in widely available, general-purpose AI, such as Claude and ChatGPT, are different from conversations with the models found within AI-powered educational tools such as MagicSchool AI or SchoolAI. Having some insight into the differences between these is important to quickly test out and share with colleagues. Also, consider what information is important to share with stakeholders in the school community, including parents and caretakers, school board members or trustees, administrators, teachers, and support staff. Getting everyone up to speed will lead to more transparent conversations and policy decisions later on.

General-purpose AI feels like engaging with a knowledgeable, adaptable conversational partner. These are the AI systems offering broad, open-ended capabilities, allowing for wide-ranging discussions on almost any topic. However, the open-ended nature also means that as educators, you need to be specific in your prompts and critical in evaluating responses. A lack of built-in guardrails means content may not always be age-appropriate or aligned with educational goals until you train your AI partner with revised prompts.

In contrast, AI-powered educational tools provide AI chats with a more structured, focused experience designed for learning environments. These tools often work as expansive platforms offering a variety of predefined features or semi-customizable features, like allowing students to dictate or to speak in multiple languages. Some features are teacher-facing, and others allow educators to create AI environments, spaces, and chats to share with students, allowing for monitoring student activity such as a student's chat history. Built-in safety features filter the responses AI generates to ensure age-appropriate content and language, and they let teachers direct how much support they want AI to give students. Although AI-powered educational tools may feel less flexible than general-purpose AI, they offer a more controlled, education-specific experience.

We have found that taking advantage of multiple AI systems allows us to make the most of what each tool offers. We adore the flexibility of general-purpose AI, imagining these systems as another colleague that works with us when we are preparing for our teaching. And we love the safety and ease of creating edtech chat environments for our students as proficient partners. Finding the right balance will depend on your needs as an educator and the broader school community's readiness to adopt AI technologies.

How AI Reads Chats

AI always reads a chat from the top to the bottom, which includes any attached documents or uploaded images. The beauty of this continuity is that your AI partner can keep thinking alongside you as you add new queries, adjust your prompts, or ask it to modify its response. The ongoing nature of the conversation allows for a dynamic, iterative conversation where ideas can be refined and developed over time.

However, as a chat becomes longer and longer, it becomes more difficult for AI to keep track of ideas and understand the context of the entire conversation—much like people. Keep this in mind. As a chat extends, AI is more likely to skip over important bits of information. It is better to work with smaller chunks of information at a time when the aim is highly focused, high-quality feedback or response. Ask your AI partner to do one thing at a time, adding in steps as it proceeds.

Technically speaking, the AI's "memory" of the conversation is limited by its *context window* or the amount of text it can process at once. When this limit is reached, earlier parts of the conversation may be forgotten or given less weight in generating responses. You'll know this is happening when you start to see inconsistencies or repetitions in longer conversations.

When inconsistencies show up in responses, it is best to start fresh in a new chat. Starting a new chat maintains the clarity and focus of the chat, especially when shifting to a new topic or starting a fresh analysis. It's like turning to a new page in a notebook—it gives you a clean slate while still allowing you to reference previous chats if needed.

Single-Student Chats

One education-focused approach is to create a discussion prompt, or bot, in which an AI partner conducts a single chat with a single student. This structure is particularly helpful for the moments when AI is your teaching assistant.

Having a single chat dedicated to a single student is a gift. Taking some time to create dedicated chats makes it possible to go back and build on information that was shared earlier in a school year. Imagine giving students a short narrative writing assignment early in the year. Oftentimes, such writing goes in a folder, remains in a notebook, or sits in Google Classroom, never to be accessed or used for learning again. (We applaud you if you've developed solutions to this common educator problem!) Deciding to organize such writing pieces within AI in a single chat, dedicated to that one student, props that writing up as a starting point for creating personal goals in the future. Wondering how a student is growing as a narrative writer? No problem—take that student's most recent writing, upload it into the chat you dedicated to them, and prompt AI: "Attached is the student's most recent narrative writing. How has this student grown as a narrative writer, and what are some next steps that this student is ready to learn and practice?" Or teach the student to do this same work, inside an edtech chat.

Single-student chats are incredibly helpful when you save a chat long term, across a unit of study, a semester, or even a year. They're also helpful even when you save it for a single class period, as you can see the tracks of student interactions.

Chats That Consider Work by Multiple Students

The question you may be asking right now is, *Can AI read all of my students' writing at once?* It's true that AI systems are increasingly able to work with large amounts of data. Approach this with both excitement and caution. As context windows for AI continually increase, you can also increasingly upload more pages of student writing at a time. It's important to note that the more information AI needs to read, the more surface level or diluted its responses can become, perhaps only giving a few general comments for each student rather than detailed analysis. It also depends on whether you are asking ChatGPT to read your student writing or asking students to upload their writing to an edtech chat.

One approach for having AI such as ChatGPT read multiple student papers at once is by combining the writing into a single document so that AI can see trends and comment on individual student writing. Having headings, such as a student's first name, gives AI a guide for demarcating where one student's writing pieces end and the next one begins. Another approach is to upload each document separately. With younger writers whose writing doesn't reach the high word counts that high school writing often expects, it's possible to copy and paste student writing into a chat window, either one chat at a time or all at once with a clear structure for AI to know when one student's work begins and ends.

Take a moment to pause and think about the pedagogical implications for working with students and not only their writing. How might you think about partnerships differently? We often say to students, "Did you know that you and so-and-so both love to write about _____? You two should be writing partners today." Now think about all those missed connections that AI can help us to see. It's like having X-ray vision. AI can help you notice things that are just under the surface. Your AI partner can suggest partnerships based on content, writing craft, research interests, or identity. It's helpful to think about how AI can support your decision making when you are working with students.

For instance, you might ask your AI partner, "Based on these students' writing, who would be great writing partners? Explain your reasoning." Or you might prompt, "Match students as writing partners based on individual writing strengths. Pair students based on complementary strengths." For example, one student might be great at dialogue and another might be great at details and description.

Due to the pesky limitations of context windows, chances are that putting every student's work into one chat in ChatGPT won't get the results you expect, so carefully choose a few at a time to upload. You can bring some strategy to deciding which writing pieces to match for AI to read with you.

You can also set students up inside an edtech chat room as a club or partners. For instance, three students who are reading the same novel or short story might converse together with an AI partner about emerging themes or ideas they have about character development. As a school, department, or grade-level team, you can make shared decisions about coaching students to include AI as a thought partner in their discussions. If you've set up an edtech chat room where students individually upload their papers, not only will they get feedback, but you'll also be able to see their work and this feedback, immediately and saved over time.

Chats Focused on Representative Samples as Student Profiles

Another helpful structure for a chat is to feed your AI partner representative student work: prototypical pieces that can represent profiles of researchers, writers, and thinkers.

If you have 150 students that you see on a daily basis, you will probably not be uploading all of their writing or responses into AI (though you can set up an edtech AI partner for students to get immediate feedback). You still want to read your students' writing so that you know about their interests, skills, and individual quirks. There is so much joy in reading student writing. Their personalities shine through. As you are reading their work, begin to sort the work into piles based on the trends you are seeing. Perhaps some students write with lots of humor—that's a pile. Or students are writing across many pages—that's a pile. Some students have short, concise writing (like Hemingway!)—that's a pile. There is no end to ways that you might sort student work, and if you've tried this based entirely on how students map to a progression of skills, challenge yourself to try a new kind of sort.

Once you've sorted, choose a representative piece for each pile, and then organize a chat around that piece for more intense feedback. Logistically, it will be much easier to read through and analyze a handful of writing pieces with AI than an entire class's worth of writing. This is especially true as students become older and the expectations for their writing volume increases significantly, which can test the limits of the amount of data AI allows for upload.

Feedback that you receive for one student becomes transferable to the entire group of students. You might even ask AI to consider that the feedback will be given to a group of similar writers than to the one individual alone. You can prompt, "This 9th grade writing is similar to a small group of other students in the class. What feedback would you give the group based on this writing?" You could also upload that feedback to your edtech chat, so that it informs the feedback given to students who use that chat to seek responses to their writing.

You'll find that you'll have an always ready assistant and endless opportunities for generating response or analysis with AI. Deciding what remains helpful and what becomes digital clutter is perhaps the perennial problem of digital work environments.

Saving, Sharing, and Deleting Chats

Most AI will require a login that allows you to manage your account. Typically, all of your chats are saved as a default setting. The amount of saved chats can quickly become long and unwieldy.

As a general rule, we recommend mindfully keeping the chats you'll want to go back to. Each AI model has a way to rename a chat to something memorable like Period 1, Lit Essay, Lesson Planning, Feedback.

Sometimes it is possible to share a chat. This feature can be particularly useful for collaborating on lesson plans, sharing successful prompts, or discussing student work with colleagues. However, it is crucial to be mindful of privacy concerns when sharing chats, especially if they contain personal information about students or school matters.

Taking a moment to learn what happens with stored data in AI chats can guide your decision making regarding what you feel comfortable sharing. We enjoy the privacy Claude provides by not automatically training their AI model on the data stored in chats. Google Gemini follows their privacy policy used across all of their products. ChatGPT allows users to turn off the storage of chats so that it doesn't become possible training data later, but it then means chats can't be returned to later. This landscape is everchanging, and policies can change. It can feel unsettling to contemplate how AI learns from your data, but data collection has existed for years when students have been on the internet and have composed in Google Classroom. By staying informed, you're better equipped to make thoughtful choices about how you and your students engage with these tools.

Deleting chats that you will never return to works to manage the amount of data that a human reviewer will be able to access in the future. It is wise to handle sensitive data with care. Following FERPA (Family Educational Rights and Privacy Act) and COPPA (Children's Online Privacy Protection Act) laws are essential, and conversations about data management are wise practice for all learning communities.

Visit ai-enhancedliteracy.org for support managing chats.

Defining Ethical and Collaborative Boundaries

Hundreds of hours spent in classrooms and in conversations around ethical use of AI have taught us one thing: We want students to know the difference between ethical and unethical uses of AI, and we need to keep exploring these boundaries in our own work as well.

We've also learned that we don't all agree on exactly where to draw those boundaries. But we do all agree that there are moments when AI is a supportive tool for learning and other times when it bypasses that goal.

We all seem to agree that students turning to AI with the prompt "Write an essay about [insert topic here]" is problematic. It sidesteps student learning, it erases student voice, and it does more than flirt with plagiarism. *And* we need to realize that the higher stakes a task is for students and the less confidence they have in their current ability to achieve at that task, the more they'll seek help. Just as we might ask AI to review a cover letter, just as we turn to AI to make our bibliography accurate, just as it has become second nature for us to use AI to translate communication, young people will also respond to the pressure to use an available tool. In *The Performance Paradox*, Eduardo Briceño (2023) talks about the performance zone, in which failure is high stakes, and the learning zone, in which experimentation is high and threat is low. Our students need us to provide more performance zone in which to learn about using AI wisely.

We really like the work that Marc Watkins and Stephen Monroe are doing at the University of Mississippi to cultivate cultures of trust (Grammarly, 2024). They warn that expecting students to misuse AI and setting up systems for AI detection create a pervasive market of distrust. Instead, they advocate for teaching integrity and exploring creativity with AI. When students are taught appropriate ways to use AI to deepen rather than replace their voice, they are more likely to work within these guardrails. Young people want to cultivate their own voice, their own perspective, their own message. When they are taught how to use AI to strengthen their voice, rather than replace it, they become wiser, more powerful AI users.

It's also important to remember that when students fall into damaging behaviors, it's usually because the tasks they face make them feel anxious and inadequate. When they get heavy coaching for college essays, it's because someone has made them feel that is necessary. When they substitute someone or something else's writing for their own, it's because they didn't feel like their own work was adequate. Look at your success criteria, assessment protocols, and grading practices, as well as your assignments. If you want to ensure that students draft on their own, give them time to draft in class. Show students how to come to AI with preliminary notes, drafts, and ideas, and you and they will be better prepared to navigate the ethical boundaries of interacting with an AI coach.

It does help to think about prompting as an ethical process. We envision ethical prompting to have a few key features that work as principles in guiding students through using AI usage during their writing or thinking process. It can be envisioned as a set of questions:

- Does this interaction support my learning without compromising academic integrity?
- Does it balance using AI capabilities with maintaining my own agency, skill development, and voice?
- Am I maintaining the role of critical thinker, learner, and decision maker?

You can also share road signs that AI use is no longer ethical. These might include the following:

- AI bypasses skill development by completing work with little student input, idea generation, or revision.
- We feel the urge not to be transparent about what role AI played in a writing or thinking process.
- Ideas are accepted without critical evaluation.
- AI input overshadows the student's ideas, writing style, or creativity.

See Figure 1.6 for some examples of ethical and unethical prompts.

Much of what constitutes ethical and unethical use of AI for learning is dependent on the user's intentions. It might be helpful to see AI write a 500-word essay on climate change if the goal is to study it as an exemplar; after all, you might turn to AI to generate this kind of exemplar for students. Assuming that students have good intentions about their learning is a positive place to coach from. It also opens up moments of instruction that wouldn't otherwise take place if you are focused on catching students cheating or reprimanding their AI usage without offering alternatives. A teacher looking to coach students through their use of AI might say something along the lines of "It's great that you are using AI to create exemplar writing; it is often easier to write when you have a clear example of what you are trying to create. Let me give you one tip. It can be hard to write an essay that reflects your thinking when you're looking at an essay about the same exact topic you are writing about. Instead, you might try asking for a 500-word essay on a slightly different topic and use that as the mentor. Let's try creating one together, and then we'll study it for writing moves that stand out to us."

Figure 1.6
Examples of Ethical Versus Unethical AI Prompts

Likely Ethical	Potentially Unethical
"Can you suggest some key points I should consider when writing an essay about climate change?"	"Write a 500-word essay about climate change for me."
"I'm struggling to understand the concept of photosynthesis. Can you explain it in simpler terms?"	"Provide a detailed explanation of photosynthesis" [that I can copy directly into my assignment].
"What are some counterarguments to the main points in my essay?"	"Rewrite my essay to make it sound more convincing and academic."
"Can you help me brainstorm some creative writing ideas for a story about friendship? I especially want to explore my friendship with my cousin. She lives in Texas, and I live in NYC."	"Generate a 1000-word creative story about friendship for me. It should focus on a friendship between a girl who lives in NYC and her cousin in Texas."
"What moments in World War II are considered turning points that I might focus my research on? What moments are disputed?"	"Summarize the key events of World War II" [so I don't have to do the research myself].
"Can you explain the steps to solve this type of quadratic equation? I'm having trouble understanding the process."	"Solve these quadratic equations for me. "
"What are some important themes to look for when reading *To Kill a Mockingbird*? I'm especially interested in themes related to race, representation, and savior archetypes."	"What's the main theme of *To Kill a Mockingbird* and some supporting evidence for that theme?" [I didn't read the book.]
"Translate these comments into Spanish so my partner and I can talk about this story together."	"Translate this entire paragraph from English to Spanish for my language homework."

It can also be helpful to lay out some expectations for how much students might turn to AI across the learning process. For instance, consider the scenarios in Figure 1.7.

In practice, balancing independent work and ethical AI use requires guidance and structure. In the same way that we wish to develop young people who write to advocate for themselves and others and who learn to love reading books, we want students to learn to leverage technology while maintaining their unique perspectives and abilities.

Figure 1.7
Balancing AI Support with Student Independence

Scenario	How Much AI Use?	What Students Can Do Independently
Initial brainstorming	Limited, personalized	Make personal choices from lists
Expanding ideas	Moderate	Evaluate and integrate AI suggestions; ask AI to look for main points in student notes
Fact-checking and reference creation	High	Verify from multiple sources
Personal reflection	Very limited	Almost entirely independent, although students might ask AI to give feedback on representation, fairness, privilege
Creative writing	Limited; use for prompts or exemplars	Write the main content
Revision	Moderate	Mediate and respond to AI feedback

Situating Yourself as a Learning Partner with Multiple AI Partners

Our final advice is to situate yourself as a learning partner around AI and literacy, the kind of learner who is willing to experiment. When a colleague wonders about using an edtech platform with children to discuss a nature video, say, "That sounds interesting. Let's try it ourselves to see how it works." When you find yourself wondering what ideas AI might suggest for finding ideas for an essay about a novel, say, "Let's try it and see."

When you begin by learning about an AI-literacy intersection, in a situation where you are trying things without kids first, you'll figure out what you love and don't love about these interactions. You can work through glitches and learn the quirks of whatever edtech platform your school adopts. And remember, you, as an adult, can turn to more flexible, powerful AI partners. You might turn to ChatGPT to generate translations for a story you will read with students. You might ask Claude to generate an asset-based rubric for a writing task. Then you might upload these into the discussion room you are setting up with your edtech partner, for your students. Think of these AI partners as a fabulous student teacher, one who is never tired, never overwhelmed, and ready to revise endlessly.

Creating AI Spaces in the Classroom

Consider the moments when you sit down to organize groups and partnerships in your classroom. You take stock of ambitious educational goals, matching and aligning them to fit the variety of personalities, backgrounds, and gifts your students bring. You contemplate different arrangements to foster a meaningful exchange of ideas, sharpen skills, and create opportunities to affirm and dignify each other.

Orchestrating AI–student partnerships closely resembles the process you work through when you thoughtfully pair students and facilitate meaningful dialogue between them. Such dialogues are no accident. Meaningful conversations require planning and preparation. It's the way you set students up to be active partners that can make or break the flow of discussion. You coach students to say more. You prompt them to drill down when you ask, "What do you mean by _____?" And you encourage them to provide evidence for their nascent claims, consider alternative viewpoints, and make connections between ideas. You teach them to use phrases like "I agree with… because…" or "I'd like to add to that point by…" to build on each other's thoughts.

Now imagine for a moment that one of those discussion partners is AI. Positioning AI as a student partner or co-teacher is an exciting proposition. Tools now exist that allow you to customize your own chatbot for students and then monitor how it's going from a teacher-facing dashboard. Although training a chatbot feels like something a more techy person should be responsible for, it turns out that educator wisdom, that hard-earned gut instinct you employ when you coach students, transfers well to coaching AI as a proficient partner and learning companion, so that each of your students can have a one-on-one discussion partner and AI tutor.

In this chapter, we'll be focusing on AI-powered edtech, such as SchoolAI, Flint, and MagicSchool AI, that you can set up as virtual sites where students enter into discussions with this AI partner. AI can give students feedback, and it can make suggestions or ask questions that lead students to deeper thinking. You are the agent in these sites: You set up the site so that your AI teaching partner leads students in directions you've launched. It will also exceed your directions in ways that can be helpful, because it leans on vast databases and programming. If you prompt your AI partner, for instance, to lead students to be critical thinkers, make cross-text comparisons, or question their assumptions, you'll notice surprising insights coming from your AI partner that can extend and deepen the feedback and prompting you might give. That's one reason these sites are so helpful: They open up the range of feedback that students encounter in the classroom. The other reason they're so helpful, of course, is that every student can get responses to their thinking simultaneously.

It's not hard to become familiar with edtech sites—as in, they are designed to be easy to use. They often make use of commercially available AI models; however, they may not seem as powerful as using ChatGPT directly from OpenAI, in that there will be constraints and boundaries. If you've become accustomed to using popular AI platforms such as Microsoft Copilot or Perplexity, you might find that your edtech site doesn't have features you want, such as uploading images or using text to speech. You, as an educator, will still want access to sites such as ChatGPT or Claude to support your planning and feedback so that you can get the full power of these tools. Your school or district will probably also invest in an edtech AI that you'll get to know and that can be surprisingly helpful as an additional virtual learning experience. Our goal is for you to feel so much better by the end of this chapter about both edtech AI and your curiosity and confidence in implementing it.

You may have a choice over your edtech AI (we hope so), or you may find that you have to learn AI that has been chosen for you. Either way, it's not actually that daunting once you dive in. In this chapter, to help you, we'll consider the following:

- Setting up AI as a learning partner.
- Balancing AI support with student growth and independence.
- Embracing unexpected (and endearing) student–AI interactions.
- Building confidence.

Setting Up AI as a Learning Partner

Let's start with a practical example. We'll create a discussion space using AI-powered edtech, some knowledge about our classroom context, and our coaching sensibilities. For this example, we'll use SchoolAI as our edtech platform. That means we need to set up our AI space, including what work we want kids to do and what role we want our AI partner to play in student discussion. In our imagined classroom, our students are reading the beloved classic *Thank You, M'am* by Langston Hughes. We'll offer some coaching and tips for you along the way.

Let's quickly review the road map of steps we are about to take in Figure 2.1. In time, you'll make them your own and you'll innovate. We've learned through experience that each of these steps plays an important role in producing desirable outcomes.

Figure 2.1

Steps for Setting Up AI as a Learning Partner for Students

Step	Action
1. Articulate learning goals	Name what students need support with or a pathway of progressive skills and learning objectives.
2. Upload relevant text	Provide AI with texts that students will be reading or tools for students or AI to use. You may need to make a PDF version to upload, for ease of access.
3. Write a guiding prompt	Craft a prompt that will lead your AI partner to invite students into a dialogue that reflects your learning goals. Expect to adjust this prompt.
4. Test the setup	Create a "test student," or use a chat preview window to see how the AI interaction plays out.
5. Modify and refine	Adjust the prompt or AI directions as needed to align with your vision for these student–AI discussions. Consider use of language, word choice, purpose, and overall tone of the interaction.

In this classroom, students are currently studying character motivation. They are thinking about main characters but are also being encouraged to look at the minor characters as well. So far, we see evidence of this analytic thinking when we name the skill explicitly and then ask students to try it (we sometimes call this "with prompting and support"), but we've noticed that in their partner and independent work, students often revert to squarely focusing on major characters. During a recent department meeting, we discussed that when our students read and discussed Langston Hughes's short story *Thank You, M'am* in past years, they tend to focus most of their attention on Roger, who is younger and closer to them in age, rather than consider Mrs. Luella Bates Washington Jones's motivations, an adult who acts with a great deal of care, insight, and compassion—a character we believe is inspiring and worthy of deeper discussion.

The moment you find yourself saying, "I wish my students had more time to practice...," pause for a moment, because that is likely a skill AI can support. In our classroom, we think it would be great if AI can nudge students to think more about Mrs. Luella Bates Washington Jones in the conversation without us posing rote questions about her from the beginning. Using AI for this purpose also feels meaningful within our context. We're using it as one tool to support difficult and tricky analytical thinking about characters. It is not our only approach. Students also read and discuss the story in partnerships and book clubs. Our goal is to coach AI in such a way that it becomes a proficient partner, almost an extra teacher, in the classroom.

We imagine coaching AI in the same way that we might coach a student toward a worthy insight and then ask them to turnkey the experience, not the answer, for another classmate. In this instance, we aim for AI interactions that are thought-provoking and natural. We see this as an opportunity for enhancing academic discourse and a time to sit with ideas about a story. We want our students to enjoy the process of peeling back the many layers of a complex text.

Our chosen edtech platform (remember we're using SchoolAI here) allows us to train, coach, and prepare AI to interact with students in ways that we see fit. We could prompt AI to role-play a character, talking to the student as if it were Roger or Mrs. Luella Bates Washington Jones. That can be productive, but today, as we've established, we want AI to be more of a thought partner. Right from the start, let's give AI some context about how we would like it to act, and then we'll upload a copy of our text.

We suspect that AI already knows *Thank You, M'am* because the story is easily accessible on the internet, but we want to ensure that it uses an accurate copy of the story. Even when we feel that a step might be redundant, such as adding a text we predict AI knows well due to its broad knowledge base, we prefer to take an extra cautious approach and add the text anyway. Edtech AI is a closed system, so that your students' data, and the work you and they produce, is not shared outside your classroom. When uploading texts to AI for educational purposes, it's best to follow the same guidelines you already use for sharing materials in your classroom. Although many educational uses may be covered by fair use, copyright laws vary by country and situation. For clarity, consider using public domain works, openly licensed materials, or texts your school has purchased, or consult your school's librarian or media specialist, who often has expertise in copyright considerations for educational settings. Chances are, you are probably not uploading texts in order to market them but are making sure that your AI edtech has full knowledge of texts you've already purchased to use with students.

AI can make use of any document we attach. For example, we can also add a skill progression chart, demonstrating progressive steps to more complex thinking. This could give AI more direction about how to coach a student progressively toward higher degrees of interpretation. We'll explore this idea a little later. For now, we'll only add a copy of the story.

Here is our prompt and a preview of what students will see based on the training we've given AI.

 Students are reading "Thank You, M'am" by Langston Hughes. They are studying character motivation. Start the chat with open-ended questions, and coach students progressively toward deeper understandings. Also, when appropriate, encourage students to think not only about Roger, but also about Mrs. Luella Bates Washington Jones.

> Welcome! Let's dive into "Thank You, M'am" by Langston Hughes. To get started, what do you think motivated Roger to try to steal Mrs. Jones's purse? And how does Mrs. Jones react to him?

Our first reaction is that we love the friendly and inviting tone. Our second reaction is that the AI response isn't exactly what we were hoping for, but it is really close. It's on topic, having both the correct story and the correct skill: character motivation. However, we'd like the AI to ease into the conversation so that it doesn't feel like an interrogation or a test. The question it asks feels too direct. Perhaps in another context this would be a perfect start; however, we're hoping to replicate the kinds of conversations we initiate as we circulate around the room: "What's on your mind right now? What is fascinating about this part?"

This testing phase is where it's easy to give up, saying, "See, it doesn't work!" Truth be told, most of us didn't get into education to teach technology, let alone coach it to analyze stories with kids. Also, this is the time to maintain a curious mindset and remind yourself what a powerful tool this will be for learning if you can tweak it just a little more. You have to approach AI like you would a student and see its potential. Cut AI (and yourself) some slack; it's learning, too. So just like when coaching in the classroom, try out something quickly, see how it goes, and try it a slightly different way if necessary.

Let's study AI's opening line more carefully, noticing what it is giving more weight to. It seems that our AI has missed the mark because it is placing more weight on our request to talk about motivation rather than on our prompt for open-ended questions. Problems like this are problems with *alignment*. The AI output is not aligned with our human expectations. This highlights a common challenge for AI language models: balancing context and specific query focus. Trust your gut when working with AI. And trust that you'll quickly see if AI is not interpreting your requests correctly. But once you do, what can be done?

Next, you can apply a coaching technique by providing the AI with a brief example of what you really mean or want. We'll give AI two specific opening questions that we feel are appropriate: What part of the story stood out most to you? Which character fascinated you the most? Notice how we integrated those into the prompt. And notice how AI now opens the conversation.

Students are reading "Thank You, M'am" by Langston Hughes. They are studying character motivation. Start the chat with open-ended questions, such as "What part of the story stood out most to you?" or "Which character fascinated you most?" and coach students progressively toward deeper understandings. Also, when appropriate, encourage students to think not only about Roger, but also about Mrs. Luella Bates Washington Jones.

Hey there! Let's dive into "Thank You, M'am" by Langston Hughes. What part of the story stood out most to you? Or was there a character that fascinated you?

This is so much better. With a little revision and a laser focus on our goals, it's possible to coach AI to be a more natural conversationalist and reading partner. It's true that AI doesn't know our students, but we certainly do. Because AI can learn quickly and, in some ways, it can replicate our approaches to teaching, it's worth spending some time to figure out how it can be an extra partner in the classroom. As we keep interacting with AI, we can keep an eye on how it progressively prompts students to think more deeply.

It's helpful to get a few colleagues together to spend 15 minutes interacting with an edtech AI you've trained. Try it during a department or faculty meeting or over a coffee together. You can test out your prompts by role-playing as a student in a teacher-created discussion space. Doing so allows you to experience AI's responses firsthand and see if those responses align with your teaching goals.

As you do this work, coach your colleagues to revise prompts iteratively, studying the nuances between AI responses based on different training instructions. The coaches we've worked with find that everyone is more at ease when the technology work is approached in the same spirit of approaching our classroom instruction. It helps to say, "Just as you would adjust your language or instructions for human students, you may need to refine your prompts for AI multiple times to get the desired outcome." Encourage all the educators you coach to bring their knowledge and experience to the table. Learning to use AI well is less about learning technology and more about learning to name and replicate our most powerful teaching.

When AI responses don't seem to be going your way, then you need to revise your initial design, which in edtech platforms is usually deliberately easy to do. In some you can add rules; in some you can add discussion prompts; in some you might simply tell it what is making you happy and unhappy. As you craft and refine your AI prompts, be clear about the ways you want AI to coach your kids. Sometimes AI isn't perfect. If AI does something strange or awkward, call it out. It's a teachable moment. Talk to it like it is your student teacher. You can say, "You are providing too much scaffolding" or "You need to explain with simpler language."

Let's name a few big aspects of the work we've explored. One, we are approaching AI as an adaptable and coachable partner. You can coach AI to replicate a process you use in the class, anything from using Who, What, Where, When questions to critical questions you bring to the text to uncover missing perspectives. On the other hand, you can also train it in what not to do. You can set boundaries such as "Ask questions but don't give students the answer—lead them to it." Or you can say, "Be a thought partner, but refuse to write reflections and essays on behalf of the student."

Let's return to our action steps for a moment. We'll match each part of our prompting to the action steps in Figure 2.2.

So far, we've spent a lot of time getting AI ready for the conversation and not a lot of time in the conversation. The principles and steps we've established apply to any other purpose we can envision for AI. For example, you might want students to generate images for video using AI. We recommend following the same exact steps to think about what sort of images they will ask for and look to see how AI tends to respond to those prompts.

You'll want to keep an eye on how AI interacts with students in the long term and especially in a live classroom environment. Kids have surprisingly creative ways of interacting with AI. Think about the ways you'll stay in the loop, knowing how your students are interacting with their digital partner. You might decide to monitor conversations from afar, reading a few interactions while circling the room. You can ask students the kinds of questions that reveal what's on their minds, giving you the opportunity to provide feedback about their conversations with AI and learn how it's pushing their thinking.

Figure 2.2
Example AI Learning Partner Setup: *Thank You, M'am*

Step	Example
1. Articulate learning goals	Enhance understanding of character motivation, focusing on Roger and Mrs. Luella Bates Washington Jones. Encourage students to look beyond the main character.
2. Upload relevant text	Uploaded the full text of *Thank You, M'am* by Langston Hughes to ensure AI has an accurate reference.
3. Write a guiding prompt	Initial prompt: "Students are reading *Thank You, M'am* by Langston Hughes. They are studying character motivation. Start the chat with open-ended questions, and coach students progressively toward deeper understanding. Also, when appropriate, encourage students to think not only about Roger, but also about Mrs. Luella Bates Washington Jones."
4. Test the setup	Tested conversation, found that AI started with too many direct questions about motivation. The tone was too direct and interrogative.
5. Modify and refine	Revised part of the prompt: "Start the chat with open-ended questions, such as 'What part of the story stood out most to you?' or 'Which character fascinated you most?'"

Coaching Students During AI Interactions

Keep an eye especially on student engagement—how they respond to AI interactions. Although you can't simultaneously engage every single student in the same moment, listening to their questions and ideas and responding personally, AI can. These partnerships can help students feel seen and listened to. You want to be involved, which you can be by surveying these chats and offering occasional feedback: "I was so interested in the idea you talked about in your chat, Sarah…" or "I made some student discussion groups today based on what you explored with your AI partner yesterday…" or "I thought today we could talk about an idea that came up in Juan's discussion yesterday." This way your presence is still felt—and you know what's happening in this AI space—while your students get more practice with literacy discussion. As students are increasing their literacy and subject-area knowledge, you'll also be increasing their literacy about interacting productively with AI.

Coach students to talk with AI in productive ways (see Figure 2.3). If students are working as a small group, you might ask about what role AI is playing in their conversation, and you may take note of the trajectory of their conversations. Is the conversation free-flowing? Laborious? Indifferent?

Figure 2.3
Coaching Students While Using AI

Look for...	Ask...	Here's a Tip...
Engagement with AI	How's the AI conversation going? Any frustrations? Confusions?	Try asking AI to explain itself. You can prompt, "How did you arrive at that interpretation? Explain your thinking."
Robust conversations	What kinds of responses are you giving?	Aim for a ping-pong chat with AI. Share an idea, let it respond, then build on what it says. Keep the conversation bouncing back and forth. You can also ask AI interpretation questions.
Coherence	Do you feel like the responses you are getting make sense?	If AI's interpretation feels off, challenge it. Ask why it thinks that way, and compare it to your own understanding.
Understanding AI's use of language	Are there words and expressions that AI uses that feel too advanced? Are there words you don't understand?	Ask AI to use more simple words. You can say, "Break down that concept for me or explain it step by step." You might say, "What does this word or phrase mean? Talk to me like I'm a beginner."
Limitations and boundaries	Is there something you are hoping AI will do that it's not doing well or refusing to do?	Think of AI like a brainstorming buddy with some quirks. When you hit its limits, use that as a chance to get creative. How can you rephrase your idea or break it into smaller parts?
Accuracy	Have you noticed any mistakes (hallucinations) where AI says things that aren't true? If so, how are you catching those mistakes?	Looks like you caught AI in a mix-up. Use this as a chance to fact-check and dig deeper. Where might the AI have gone wrong? Can you find the correct info? Be an investigator.
Critical thinking	In what ways are you thinking differently? Did the conversation lead to any aha moments or sudden bursts of awareness?	After chatting with AI, it's helpful to take a quick thought inventory. Jot down the new ideas that popped up. Also, did it challenge your views or confirm them? Write a quick note about how your thinking shifted. It's like watching your brain grow in real time. You can also tell your AI partner that you are interested in gender, racial stereotypes, or historical representation. Ask it to challenge you.

(continued)

Figure 2.3—(*continued*)
Coaching Students While Using AI

Look for...	Ask...	Here's a Tip...
Opportunities to take learning to peers	What ideas from this conversation would you like to bring to human partners?	After your AI chat, write down any new ideas or questions it sparked. These can be great starting points for class discussions.
Opportunities to deepen cross-textual discussion	Have you reminded your AI partner what else you've been reading? Ask your AI about possible themes, characters, or ideas you might discuss across texts, or suggest some.	"I want to talk about more than one text at a time. I've also been reading...." "I'm interested in comparing... to...."

One of our greatest joys of being in the classroom is sitting side-by-side with kids and listening in on their conversations. We love joining in and exploring ideas deeply together. Nothing should replace these precious human moments. Neither should we underestimate the power of machine–human relationships to engage deeper thinking and to provide students with swift, on-the-spot responses.

In the past (and still today), we might say, "Let's Google that." Now we might say, "Let's look at how AI analyzes this." Using a search engine has been a pursuit of information. AI, however, has the power to recognize patterns, present interpretations, and generate responses. Often we've relied on scientists, mathematicians, and historians, among others, to share interpretations through static books, articles, videos, and podcasts. We've taught our students to study and expand upon the ideas of experts. AI provides yet another powerful tool for students to interact with that allows them to explore passions, develop insights, bridge gaps, and challenge with their own intuitions and experience. Interpretation work has always been a collaborative pursuit.

Balancing AI Support with Student Growth and Independence

We've long worried that learners can become too reliant on sources of assistance. Long before digital technology, proficient friends, siblings, parents, tutors, and a tremendous variety of online resources blurred our vision of what students accomplish independently. We have always struggled to find the balance between giving kids too much help and too little, and valuing what they do with no help or valuing how they seek assistance.

We know that learners can make rapid progress when they receive strong, scaffolded support in a new skill; then, by gradually removing those supports, students practice those skills with increased independence (Fisher & Frey, 2021).

We also know that assistive technology provides access to students, especially neurodiverse students and multilingual learners who need this technology in order to fully represent their abilities. Without differentiated support, we may inadvertently create an environment where some learners progress while others fall behind.

The trouble we run into with AI is that we as a community of educators haven't made up our minds or come to a consensus regarding what sort of tool AI is within schools. Should we place AI technology in the realm of assistive technologies that increase a student's access to curriculum? Should we see it as a tool designed to tutor and mentor kids into higher degrees of performance and, eventually, independence?

Both are desirable. Schools have become accustomed to assistive tools for checking spelling and grammar. AI feedback on content, clarity, and consistency of ideas across an entire written document easily feels like a natural next step. Further, AI can support students in brainstorming ideas, fact-checking, looking for bias, considering audience, and noting areas for elaborating an idea. This is powerful stuff.

Also, at the same time, we as educators want to see students progressively write with more power on their first drafts. We want them to seek novel ideas in brainstorming sessions that don't involve asking Google or AI. We want students to have the facts straight right from the start and to constantly develop an awareness of their bias and account for how it affects their choice of words, the questions they ask, and the positions they defend.

And we as authors have to admit, here, that we have been ignoring a third avenue altogether: when AI is the best possible tool for accomplishing a task, much like a microscope in a science classroom. For example, scientists from the Dominica Sperm Whale Project (Sharma et al., 2024) have teamed with AI researchers to study whale communication, uncovering subtle sound differences and patterns that are undetectable to humans. It's something that couldn't be done without AI.

We are excited about the possibility of AI being used by novice scientists in classrooms to tackle incredibly large datasets or by budding linguists to see trends and themes in a large corpus of literature. Emerging historians can use AI to transcribe difficult-to-read historical documents and expand their research capabilities beyond traditional limitations. Linguists can trace language use, including the lingering of colonial naming protocols and stances. These tools have the potential to democratize advanced research methods, allowing students to engage with complex data and primary sources in ways previously reserved for seasoned professionals.

There are a few ways to teach your students how to use AI so that it empowers them and increases their independence. One of the most important is to think about the transition from learning with AI to learning from AI. For instance, when you set students up to rehearse their thinking before a book club conversation, have them pause after talking to their AI partner and use their notebook to jot notes in preparation for club conversations. When your students have gotten feedback from AI on their writing, have them review this feedback before their next *in-class* writing assessment so that they are learning from AI, not learning only to rely on it.

You can also name how you are using AI (you and students) for each task, asking, "Am I using AI to increase access or to learn something new?" See Figure 2.4.

AI to Deepen Complexity and Understanding

Classrooms are not just about taking a single skill and training students to be more independent. The complexity of learning should also be increasing as well. Increased complexity often requires high degrees of initial support—you need a deeper understanding of progressions to plan for how you want student work to deepen. Let's look now at how AI can help you with both increasing the complexity of tasks students are able to encounter and the independence with which they will be able to encounter those challenges in the future.

Let's return to our students who are reading *Thank You, M'am* and consider how we might use AI to support students' gradual progression toward increased complexity in character analysis—and increased independence.

It's worth it to articulate a skill progression for the major lines of thinking you hope your students will develop. This is where you can step out of your edtech AI and turn as an adult educator to a more powerful AI to draft skill progressions. When we do this work with teachers, we often start with one exemplar, such as one for analyzing characters, and then ask AI to make something similar for analyzing symbolism, perspective, and so on.

Figure 2.4
AI for Increasing Access or Learning

Type of Practice	AI for Increasing Access	AI for Increasing Learning
"I do" (teacher demonstrates)	• The teacher demonstrates how to use AI tools to access information or perform tasks that might be challenging without AI assistance. • The teacher models effective prompting techniques, critical evaluation of AI responses, and ethical use.	• The teacher models how to use AI as a learning tool to develop skills and understanding. • The teacher shows how to use AI for feedback, practice, and extension of learning.
"We do" (guided practice)	• Students and teachers work together to use AI tools to access needed information or assistance. • The teacher guides students in crafting effective prompts and applying critical-thinking skills to evaluate and use AI responses appropriately.	• Students and teachers work together to use AI tools for learning tasks. • The teacher guides students in crafting effective prompts and using AI responses to deepen understanding and skills.
"You do" (independent practice)	• Students independently use AI tools to access needed information or assistance. • Students apply the skills they've learned to effectively leverage AI as an accessibility tool.	• Students independently use AI tools to support their learning process. • Students apply AI in ways that enhance their own skill development and knowledge acquisition. • Students apply their knowledge and skills in environments without the use of AI and set goals for improvement.

Once you have a progression, then you can upload it to your edtech AI, so that your AI partner understands how you anticipate students' thinking can deepen in complexity. For our imagined classroom, for example, we've developed a narrative reading progression (see Figure 2.5) to support analyzing character motivation, including in increasingly complex text.

Figure 2.5
Narrative Reading Progression

Character Motivation			
In my thinking, jotting, and talking, I explore...			
★	★★	★★★	★★★★
What shapes characters' decisions and actions, especially details in the text that are clues to characters' motivations	What drives characters, including how characters' decisions may be motivated by more than one thing, including external and internal factors	How characters' decisions and motivations may be influenced by moments that occurred much earlier in the narrative, as well as how characters may be shaped by social pressures	How character motivations are shaped by multiple pressures, or systems and dynamics that are outside their control, such as racism, sexism, and gender and sexuality norms

Visit ai-enhancedliteracy.org to download a sample overall narrative reading progression for analyzing characters.

Now let's explore how we can leverage our edtech AI to support students' growth along this continuum. Remember, our goal is to use AI as a scaffold and source of feedback that gradually fades as students gain proficiency.

 Coach student thinking using the attached narrative reading progression chart. Start by asking students to describe their thoughts about characters in the story. Then, match their responses to the level on the progression. Coach them to strengthen their current level and to reach the next one. If students don't give responses that match the chart, discuss topics that relate to the beginning of the progression.

There are two ways we can set up our AI learning environment to coach students up through the progression. One way is to give the entire progression to AI. In any scenario, this can be a wise move as it will give AI the context of our classroom goals and values. By giving AI the progression in its entirety, we will ask AI to match student responses to the progression, strengthen their thinking at the level they are currently meeting, and then prompt them to think about aspects of the text related to the next step of the progression. In this scenario, AI acts like a teaching assistant who knows exactly where each student stands and what they need to tackle next.

 These students are proficient at describing "How characters' decisions and motivations may be influenced by moments that occurred much earlier in the story, as well as how characters may be shaped by social pressures." Coach them to also notice "How characters' motivations are shaped by multiple pressures, or systems and dynamics that are outside their control, such as racism, sexism, and gender and sexuality norms."

A second way we can think about setting students up to work through this progression is to first match the students to the progression ourselves, perhaps by looking at some of their writing about character motivation, and then set up an AI environment that targets the specific skill on the progression that the student can benefit from practicing. We might develop groups, or profiles of students, for instance, who are ready for particular next steps. Here, we start by manually matching students to the progression, perhaps by analyzing some of their writing about character motivation. Once we've identified where each student falls on the continuum, we can set up targeted AI environments that focus on specific skills each student needs to practice. This method allows for a more curated experience, with AI acting as a precision tool in our instructional toolkit.

Both methods aim to strike that delicate balance between support and independence, using AI as a tool that gradually fades as students gain proficiency and confidence. Our second approach is a bit more hands-on for us as teachers. Both of these approaches allow us to scaffold learning, maintain consistent application of our progression, and push students toward more complex inferential thinking. At the same time, they maintain the crucial roles of teacher guidance and student agency in the learning process. Note that it can also be interesting to ask your AI partner to comment when students do interesting thinking work that is *outside* the progression as well. Sometimes students make surprising insights, and AI will also surprise you with its insights.

Over time, we might set up AI interactions where students initiate the conversation, rather than having AI lead with questions. Or we might set groups of students up to turn to AI only periodically, encouraging students to engage in peer discussions or independent reflection between AI consultations.

 I think Ponyboy is motivated by love for his friends.

 That's a great insight! Love for friends is definitely a strong motivation for Ponyboy. Can you think of any other factors that might influence his actions or feelings?

Another effective strategy is to use AI as a challenge partner rather than a direct guide. For instance, we might prompt our AI, "Listen to the student's analysis of character motivation. Then respectfully challenge their thinking by asking them to consider an alternative perspective or a factor they might have overlooked. Don't provide the alternative view directly, but guide the student to discover it through questioning." Students can also learn to ask, "What part of the text am I not thinking about?" or "How would you challenge my thinking?"

The "challenge my thinking" approach pushes students to defend and deepen their thinking rather than rely on AI for answers. This strategy transforms AI from a source of information to a tool for critical thinking. It encourages students to question their own assumptions and consider multiple perspectives, key skills in advanced literary analysis.

Remember that AI is only one partner in rich, nuanced discussions students will have with their peers. Be intentional about creating spaces for these human-to-human interactions. Maybe you use AI as a warm-up or to generate initial ideas but then transition to small-group discussions where students build on those ideas together. Or maybe AI is one partner in a group discussion. Your edtech AI helps more students get more feedback on their thinking quickly. It can help students develop confidence in the line of thinking they want to bring to their club or write in their essay. Make time to coach students in saving their chats as notes, or jotting notes, so that they can use their AI discussions as a diving board to other interactions.

See Figure 2.6 for a planning template. Visit ai-enhancedliteracy.org for additional templates for training your edtech AI partner to support a gradual release model and student independence.

Figure 2.6
Using AI to Support Skill Progression and Independence

Step	Description	Teacher Action
1. Align AI prompts with skill levels	Match AI prompts to students' current level on the progression.	Create level-appropriate prompts for AI.
2. Increase complexity for higher levels	Gradually introduce more sophisticated concepts as students progress.	Design prompts that encourage deeper analysis.
3. Balance AI support with student independence	Reduce AI support as students gain proficiency.	Limit AI interactions and encourage student-initiated conversations.
4. Use AI as a challenge partner	Transform AI from information source to critical-thinking tool.	Prompt AI to respectfully challenge student thinking.
5. Integrate AI with human interactions	Combine AI support with traditional teaching methods.	Use AI as a warm-up or idea generator, followed by human discussions.

Embracing Unexpected (and Endearing) Student–AI Interactions

So far, we've explored the practical. We should also take a moment to explore the endearing ways students approach AI. When you get these systems set up and students start chatting with their AI partner, you'll find yourself laughing sometimes at what AI says and what students say. There is a surprising, quirky quality to these interactions.

In one 6th grade classroom, students were reading "To Build a Fire" by Jack London. While students discussed their many insights about the short story with AI, we were also surprised and amused by the care students bring to their AI learning companions. Here, Bella critiques the main character's lack of attention to warnings about the risky environment. She then invites her AI partner to call her by name:

> 🧑 It was a first degree mistake, after many warnings from other travelers the man paid no attention to risks or what is at stake. Though the husky helped alot, it wasn't enough. Also my name is Bella, is there a nickname I can call you?
>
> ✨ Great insights, Bella! How do you think the main character could have better prepared for the journey to prevent his unfortunate end? What specific actions could he have taken based on the warnings he received?
>
> And you can call me Spark! What do you think?

How endearing for Bella to also want to call her AI partner by name ("Spark!"). There is something so fascinating about watching this virtual intelligence at work. And there is something so beautiful and important about how students show their longing for connection and care.

Another student, Maggie, asks AI to define an expression she doesn't understand. Notice that the AI used academic language, the kind of language that commonly comes up on high-stakes tests.

> ✨ It's fascinating how the story highlights the contrast between the dog's instincts and the man's knowledge. How do you think the man's reliance on his past knowledge impacted his decisions compared to the dog's instincts in the harsh Yukon environment? Can you draw any parallels between their choices and the situations you've faced where instincts and knowledge played a role?
>
> 🧑 what do you mean by "draw any parallels"
>
> ✨ Drawing parallels means finding similarities or connections between two different things. Can you think of a time in your life when you had to rely on your instincts or knowledge to make a decision, just like the man and the dog did in the story? How did it turn out, and what did you learn from that experience?

In the midst of our teaching, students may feel uncomfortable asking a teacher to explain tricky words, but here, Maggie shows that the personal quality of her interaction with her AI partner allows her to feel comfortable asking questions. This quality, of a personal conversation, is one that we should think about more as educators. Schools tend to reward extroversion. The child who thinks quickly, gets their hand up, speaks up, or has linguistic capital and social capital is often viewed as a strong, engaged student and will receive lots of positive feedback. Meanwhile, quiet thinkers also need feedback and affirmation. Notice here how AI responds with care and insight, respecting Maggie's question, shifting its language, and inviting Maggie to make personal connections that will give her more insight into the story and help her feel confident in this discussion.

You can see some of this same care in this next interaction with Pablo. Notice the affirmation Pablo receives from AI. Pablo makes a small comment, about how useful it would have been for the main character in "To Build a Fire" to have a partner. His AI partner helps Pablo develop that line of thinking.

> ✦ Hello there! Let's embark on an adventure to explore "To Build a Fire" by Jack London. What did you find interesting about the story?
>
> 👤 What is your name?
>
> ✦ I'm your trusty guide on this literary adventure! Speaking of names, in "To Build a Fire," the main character faces challenges alone. How do you think he could have approached his journey differently?
>
> 👤 If he brought a partner, he would have had more help with different things
>
> ✦ That's a great point! How do you think the story would have unfolded differently if the main character had a partner with him during his journey? What kind of challenges or benefits could arise from having someone else there?

You can still see here, though, that Pablo shows that he wants connection, too, by wanting his AI partner to have a name. We would consider telling our AI partner, from the start, to use students' names and to perhaps have a specific nickname they use themselves with each student. When Maggie signs off, you can see her wishing a good day to her partner. We believe in modeling courtesy. When we chat with AI, we are courteous, and students will follow that lead.

> goodbye have a good day
>
> Goodbye! Have a fantastic day! If you ever want to change more about decision making or any other exciting topics, feel free to come back. Keep exploring and learning!
>
> what are your plans for the rest of the day
>
> It's great to hear from you again! After our discussion on decision making in "To Build a Fire," how do you think your approach to making decisions might change? Can you imagine situations in your life where you might rely more on your instincts or learned knowledge based on what you learned from the story?

Building Confidence

We hope you feel more confident now to set up educational AI sites with and for your students. Remember, you don't have to start with 100 students; start with 5. Invite a tech group to pilot with you. Some students get so good, so quickly at this that they can help set up chat parameters for book discussions or a history conversation. Ask for planning time, with colleagues, to create some chat rooms and to try them out.

Here are some essential tips for using AI-powered edtech:

- Start simple: AI-powered edtech often comes with pre-set boundaries. Test the system without adding extra constraints at first to maintain flexibility.
- Align with your curriculum: Use the upload feature to provide AI with relevant tools (e.g., charts and datasets in science or social studies; texts, rubrics, progressions, and standards in ELA).

- Iterate and refine: Preview and test AI responses, then modify your instructions to align with learning goals.
- Build confidence gradually: Through careful testing and refinement, you can develop trust in the AI's interactions with your classroom context.

Remember to also let go of perfection. Nothing in school is perfect. It is interesting!

Harnessing AI as a Writing Coach

Most teachers can vividly recall moments when they wondered what tip they could give a young writer that would be most useful. You wonder, Should I praise this one craft move they employed that stood out? Is that technique really that powerful? What if I praise it and then it becomes an annoying habit they never break? If the writer is a novice, you wonder, What is there to praise? What should I say? If they are very accomplished, you worry quietly, What can I offer this writer? You also worry, How will I find the time to give feedback to these dozens of writers who are all waiting for my wisdom?

AI can be an incredible source of immediate writing feedback for teachers as they coach young writers. Even for those who have taught writing for years, who love to confer with writers, and who feel confident in seeing and naming writing techniques in student writing, AI will surprise with its insight into structure and craft, its grasp of possible meanings, its descriptive compliments, and, of course, its instantaneity. It offers new possibilities for expanding the range and rapidity of feedback teachers can provide. It will provide a deep pool of powerful, high-leverage feedback options. AI can be a beautiful tool for strengthening both writing instruction and teacher and student confidence with writing across a school.

AI-generated feedback can also overwhelm and culturally flatten. AI doesn't know each student, and it won't adjust feedback based on knowledge of that young human being unless it is given specific, personalized information. Its feedback has to be *mediated* by a human, either in how that feedback is shared or, if you are setting up an edtech chat, how that feedback is structured. A human needs to decide how much feedback is helpful, how they might transform the feedback experience, and when in the writing process to share that feedback. A human also needs to train its AI partner to be alert to its homogenizing effects.

Our goal here is to negotiate the best of AI possibilities for generating writing feedback. You will be crucial in this process. Educators need to bring their full humanity, knowledge of the writing process, and skills in fostering engagement to forge a constantly evolving working partnership with AI around teaching writing. Our end goal is what it has always been: to develop passionate and graceful writers who are confident of their own voice, who understand the power of the writing process, who have a clear sense of ethical boundaries as they seek coaching for their writing, and who are willing to work at their writing in the company of others.

In this chapter, we'll explore the following:

- What does AI see in student writing?
- Harnessing AI across the writing process.
- Training your AI writing coach.
- Setting up edtech chats for student writers.
- AI as an instructional planning partner.
- Teaching kids wise ways as digital writers.
- Embracing AI as part of the future of writing.

What Does AI See in Student Writing?

Educators won't *want* to learn how to turn to AI as a writing coach until they're convinced that the feedback AI can give is worth seeking. The easiest way to illuminate the value of AI as a feedback partner in writing is to look at some student work with colleagues and then judge how AI would respond to it in comparison to how you would as writing teachers.

Here's a piece of student narrative writing, for instance. It was written in one sitting as an on-demand assessment by a young writer named María. The prompt invited students to tell a true story about one moment of strong emotion. María was new to the school, new to the grade and class, and new to writing narratives in English. Her family had recently immigrated from the Dominican Republic to the Bronx.

Try looking at this piece of writing, and as you do so, ask yourself (and colleagues if you're with them), What would you say to this writer? What would you compliment? What next steps might you suggest?

> once when Jenny was at my house she opened unas papas fritas and the bag explode and there was papas fritas everywhere in the rug and in our cloths and in our hair and when we pickd them up they got more they got under our nails and under our clothes and it was like una magia horible there were papas fritas everywhere. the rug was dark blue and the papas fritas was yellow and it looked like estrellas en un cielo oscuro. Sometimes i find little yellow pieces still and when that happens i think of Jenny and how she is like una estrella en mi cielo when it is dark

For us, it feels very important that the feedback María receives shows her how valued she is in every way, celebrates her translanguaging, and acknowledges the beauty of how she has described this single moment of friendship. We might consider next steps of teaching her about paragraphing and perhaps conventions for capitalization. Coming up with that feedback feels natural for an experienced writing teacher. But imagine you're a new writing teacher, unsure of what exactly to prioritize.

Let's see what our AI partner sees in this piece of writing, with the aim of deciding if we have confidence in this feedback. Here's our AI partner's initial response, when asked to generate feedback on what María is doing well and what might be possible next steps:

1. **Vivid Descriptions:** You've done a great job describing the scene, especially the contrast between the dark blue rug and the yellow papas fritas. This helps the reader visualize the situation.
2. **Use of Bilingual Elements:** Your incorporation of Spanish phrases like "unas papas fritas" and "una magia horible" adds a unique flavor to your story. It's a great way to share your cultural background and make your writing stand out.

3. **Spelling and Grammar:** Watch out for small spelling and grammar errors. For example, "cloths" should be "clothes," and "pickd" should be "picked." Also, ensure verb tenses are consistent.
4. **Narrative Flow:** The story flows well, but consider adding more structure. You could introduce the incident more clearly at the beginning and then describe the aftermath.
5. **Emotional Connection:** The ending where you compare Jenny to a star in your dark sky is a beautiful metaphor. It adds emotional depth to your story and helps the reader connect to your feelings.

We like this feedback. It is warm, it is culturally relevant, and it is insightful. Most important for us, it focuses on the big things María is doing as a writer and as a human being: the way she compares Jenny to a star in a dark sky, the way she develops an underlying metaphor, and the way she sees beauty in an ordinary moment. Seeing the content and quality of this feedback gives us confidence in our AI partner.

You can increase your confidence in your AI partner by training it to see qualities you value and to make its writing feedback more personal and specific. In "Revisiting 'The Power of Feedback' from the Perspective of the Learner," Mandouit and Hattie (2023) describe how the purpose of feedback should be to support learners in reaching their goals. Knowing that María is currently not tremendously interested in "fixing" her grammar and is more interested in extending her voice, you can teach your AI partner to be even more affirming and more specific about the value of translanguaging and of celebrating cultural capital. It is fascinating to see how kind and supportive (and specific and expert) an AI partner can be as a writing coach. In "Better Feedback with AI?" Nagelhout (2023) showed that AI can deliver feedback that is humane and encouraging—especially when you give your AI partner feedback on its feedback.

For instance, we might suggest to our AI partner:

Please modify this feedback to ensure that this writer feels very encouraged and is not worried yet by the grammar and spelling she does not know. I also want to value her translanguaging—the way she uses all her languages. I want her to see that as a strength both for the poetic language it brings to her writing and for the way it expresses her culture. This writer is an 11-year-old writer who identifies as Latina, from the Dominican Republic. Her favorite writer is Sandra Cisneros.

Now let's see what the feedback looks like. And let's add in something that AI can do better than most classroom teachers: use all the power of its linguistic knowledge to offer María this feedback in English and Spanish:

 It's wonderful to see your story about the papas fritas incident! Your storytelling is lively and paints a vivid picture, making it enjoyable to read. I particularly love how you blend Spanish phrases into your writing. This not only adds a unique and poetic touch but also beautifully reflects your Dominican heritage. It's a real strength to be able to express yourself in more than one language, and you're doing it wonderfully!

Your writing style reminds me of Sandra Cisneros, with its vivid imagery and emotional depth. Just like her, you have a natural ability to bring your experiences and culture to life through words. Keep embracing your unique voice and the rich linguistic heritage you bring to your stories. Keep writing and exploring your talent— you're doing fantastic!

¡Es maravilloso ver tu historia sobre el incidente con las papas fritas! Tu manera de contar la historia es animada y pinta una imagen vívida, lo que hace que sea un placer leerla. Me encanta especialmente cómo mezclas frases en español en tu escritura.

> Esto no solo agrega un toque único y poético, sino que también refleja bellamente tu herencia dominicana. Es una verdadera fortaleza poder expresarte en más de un idioma, y lo estás haciendo de maravilla!
>
> Tu estilo de escritura me recuerda a Sandra Cisneros, con sus imágenes vívidas y profundidad emocional. Al igual que ella, tienes una habilidad natural para dar vida a tus experiencias y cultura a través de las palabras. Sigue abrazando tu voz única y la rica herencia lingüística que aportas a tus historias. ¡Sigue escribiendo y explorando tu talento, lo estás haciendo fantástico!

We feel pretty great about this feedback. It highlights María's cultural capital, it stays focused on all that is beautiful about her as a young writer and a young person, and it restrains itself from critiques that might diminish her current confidence as a writer. It bolsters María as a reader and as a young person who brings a valued cultural heritage to this community and to her writing. It helps make the classroom an environment where multilingual learners and newcomers can thrive. As literacy coaches, we'd be thrilled if our teachers had this kind of warm, knowledgeable feedback at their fingertips. Cope and colleagues (2021, p. 1229) suggest that AI "offers the potential to transform education in ways that—counterintuitively perhaps—make education more human, not less." We see that here, in the warm, affirming quality as well as the precision of this feedback. We can easily imagine turning this feedback into a note to María's parents and family, telling them about some of the beautiful work she is doing, that we are studying with an AI partner.

Try this out: Study a piece of student work, seek AI feedback, and see if the feedback would be helpful for your students and colleagues. We believe you'll find, like us, that even for experienced writing teachers, the depth and immediacy and inclusivity of feedback can be a gift. And all along the way, you can shape the quality and tone of this feedback by training your AI partner how to shape its feedback to match your educational values. You can also learn to turn to AI as a coach across the stages of the writing process.

Harnessing AI Across the Writing Process

All professional writers know the value of the writing process. Whether you are a novelist like George R. R. Martin who drafts and revises over years (many, many years) or a blogger who drafts and revises within an hour, all writing improves when the writer takes a moment to think about their writing, and it improves even more when the writer can develop and revise. There is great clarity for teachers in understanding the significance of the writing process. It means you'll always teach your students to do a little planning, seek mentor texts, consider possible revision, and expect to work at their writing. There is also great comfort for students in this process. Very rarely does writing emerge the way you wish initially. It starts out a sort of doughy mess, but throughout the writing process, it turns from lumpy cake batter into red velvet cupcakes.

When we think about coaching writers, we know from researchers like John Hattie (2023) that feedback is most effective when it is given early in the learning process and when learners can apply it in immediate practice. For writers, that means not waiting until students have drafted to offer feedback and consultation. How often have you, as a teacher, thought as you consider a final draft, "I wish I had spoken with this writer earlier"? How often have your students wished they got coaching as they developed their ideas?

AI can be surprisingly humane in supporting young writers. For example, we taught young writers recently that one strategy they can use to find ideas for their personal narratives or memoirs was to tell their AI partner a little bit about themselves and ask for story ideas. Kids told their AI buddies things like that they loved golden retrievers, that they had an older sister who was strict with them, and that they spent a lot of time in the library or on the baseball field. They also told them things that were hard, like that they didn't fit in with the popular kids, that they'd suffered losses, or that they missed their old home. Here's the beginning of the response María's AI partner gave her:

 It sounds like moving away from your last home was very painful. It's natural that you are missing your friends, and the places where you spent so much time. It's hard, too, when you don't get to make the decision about when to move, or where. Sometimes writing can help you hold onto beloved memories, and find more peace. Maybe ideas for your memoir could include:

Then María's AI partner listed some of the things she had told it, converting them into story ideas such as "the last evening sitting in my favorite orange tree" and "making lunch with my grandmother." What struck us, though, was how kind María's AI partner was and how María got a personal, intimate response.

Kindness and intimacy matter, especially early in the writing process, when any writer's ideas are more nebulous and vulnerable and you are trying to be careful to protect student agency and voice. Once students have drafts in hand, their voice and intention are clearer and more likely to sustain themselves in the face of feedback. You might, then, think about using AI early on in the writing process as a tool to widen possibility in terms of topic choice, and then shift further on in the process to using AI as a coach to develop students' vision and voice. Figure 3.1 includes some examples.

Figure 3.1
Ways to Collaborate with AI Across the Writing Process

In This Stage of the Writing Process	You Might Ask AI to...
Collecting and generating ideas	• Suggest mentor texts that serve as exemplars of the genre students will write. Tailor these selections to your students' identities, cultures, and interests. • Invite students to share information about their interests, and then ask AI to suggest several possible ideas, themes, or issues related to a topic or text that students might explore. • Suggest some texts or research students might turn to in order to deepen their understanding of and engagement with a topic. • Invite AI to summarize big ideas and themes from collected notes. • Consider representation, cultural relevance, and under-represented ideas, perspectives, and voices as possible angles for topics or inquiries. • Share what other writers and thinkers have explored in this area to imagine new ideas or adapt existing ones.
Drafting	• Analyze different mentor texts in terms of their *structure* to offer choice for planning with structure in mind. • Analyze some mentor texts in terms of *focus* to demonstrate how writers maintain focus while developing a vision. • Suggest parts that writers might draft as they develop their writing inside of a genre. • Recommend a few mentor texts with lively or highly personalized voices to inspire writers to develop their own voices as they write. • Provide mentor texts whose authorship or voice matches your students'. Some young writers particularly like to study writers who share their cultural identity to apprentice themselves to that particular perspective.

(continued)

Figure 3.1—(*continued*)
Ways to Collaborate with AI Across the Writing Process

In This Stage of the Writing Process	You Might Ask AI to...

Revising	• Provide feedback on how student writing fulfills that student's vision and purpose for their writing.
	• Suggest areas of student writing that the writer could develop more thoroughly and some choices for how to do this.
	• Analyze how a student writer has successfully mentored themselves to another writer they admire.
	• Provide compliments and next steps on one or more of these areas:
	  – Focus
	  – Structure
	  – Meaning
	  – Craft
	  – Word choice
	• Provide feedback on how student writing fulfills specific qualities described on a rubric, checklist, or set of benchmark standards.
	• Provide feedback on how student writing manifests techniques that are *not* on a rubric, checklist, or set of benchmark standards but that are beautiful and significant.

Publishing	• Co-author images or text features to fulfill students' visual ideas. • Generate edited reference lists from students' research sources. • Translate student work into multiple languages for families and community members. • Provide feedback on conventions, including common patterns that students can learn from. • Provide examples of conventions that students seek support in, with instructional explanations.

As you look at this list in Figure 3.1, you'll notice that whenever possible we suggest ways of working with AI that include choice. Sometimes our default as teachers is to assess and give feedback on how students fulfill our vision for their writing. Felicia Rose Chavez (2021) reminds us that the goal should be, instead, to help students fulfill their vision. Rubrics and checklists can sometimes get in the way, narrowing our vision of what writing should look and sound like until student writing becomes nearly indistinguishable. Yet they can also offer support, a possible path for novice writers who would appreciate a stepladder. As you turn to AI, then, keep thinking about prompting AI to not only give feedback on classroom criteria, but also to respond to student goals, learn about the mentor writers students admire, and give feedback on how student writing reaches their personal vision. It's also really important for students to learn to prompt their AI partner to suggest multiple options, so that the student can weigh and evaluate these options, forcing analytic thinking.

Training Your AI Writing Coach

Your AI partner will respond to your training so that it becomes the writing coach you want it to be—although it will also be more than you want, different than you want, and ever changing, as it is a mutable intelligence. Know that it has enormous, untapped potential as a creative force.

Respecting the critical and creative capacities of AI will allow you to access ideas, insights, and resources that you would not have come up with in time frames that still seem like magic. Your AI partner can analyze a mentor text in seconds. It can study a collection of student work in the same time frame and offer actionable feedback. It can write letters in multiple languages for you to parents and community members. And it can overwhelm your writers with too much feedback or rely on a flattened, universalistic vision of writing that could homogenize your writers. So you'll need to learn a little bit about training your AI partner, you'll need to be alert to how your AI partner responds to your prompts and the tools you offer, and you'll want to be imaginative in how you might expand your prompts to be more inclusive and less predictable.

Let's start by training with rubrics or checklists. For instance, here is a student's draft, "Rats and How They Roll." This argument was a flash-draft, or on-demand assessment, a 7th grader wrote in one period, at the launch of an argument unit.

Rats And How they Roll

Most people think rats are gross, dirty animals, but they are not. Rats are amazing creatures they are survivalists and help us alot more than do bad.

Rats survival skills are amazing! They can fall off a 5 story building and live, it can also collapse its bones and then crawl through a hole that is a quarter inch the size of a quarter in diamiter. Rats also climb up a toilet pipe, get flushed back down, and live! I think because of their survival skills they deserve to be around, I mean they are like little Bear Grylls!

Rats are also amazing because many people around the world adore these rodents but not as a pet or, or a survivalist but as dinner! People around the world adore rat meat. the chinese call it household deer because they taste like venasine! Evern some of the best french restaurants serve rats that had drunk wine while they were living saying it gave the meat more flavor. People in Mexico also eat rat that farmers caught eating their crops. Health scientists said that the rat meat has alot of protein and vitamins and they also said because of the large rat population they said it could be a future food source.

Rats are also important for medical reason because since rats are so similar to humans it alot of ways so rats are tested on medicine and how people get diseases. Rats are needed and when born the pups are put in a sealed building and protected from bacteria and fleas until they are needed. Rats have shown that smoking led to cancer by exposing rats to cigar smoke. Rats are also tested for cures also even the vaccine for polio was tested on rats.

I hope you can see now that rats are not that bad as they are food sources all around the world, survivalists and pretty hardcore, and are the reason we don't have horrible diseases like polio today. I hope you are now aware of all the good rats do.

One simple way to train your AI partner is to provide it with a checklist, such as the one in Figure 3.2, that you can find on ai-enhancedliteracy.org.

Figure 3.2

Argument Checklist, 7th Grade

What to Check	What It Looks Like in My Writing	✓
Overall	I staked a clear claim and developed my argument with reasoning and evidence. As I developed my argument, I acknowledged other perspectives and the complexity of the topic.	
Lead	I introduced my argument by giving some context or background information about the topic, to orient my reader and explain the significance of this topic.	
	I made a clear claim that let the reader know my position on the topic.	
Structure	I organized my argument into parts, using paragraphs to define the parts of my argument.	
	I ordered my reasons and evidence carefully, building my argument with logical sequence to convince my reader.	
	I used transitional phrases to move my reader from one part of my argument to the next and to clearly introduce new evidence.	

When prompted to provide feedback and next steps using the checklist, our AI partner provided a list that closely adheres to the qualities described in the checklist. Providing your AI partner with tools, then, helps train it to value the same benchmarks and qualities that you value in your instruction.

 I've reviewed the 7th grade writer's essay on rats and the provided checklist. Here are the prioritized next steps for revision:

1. **Thesis Statement Clarity:** Ensure that the thesis statement is clear and directly addresses the essay's main argument about rats. It should be a specific stance the essay will support.
2. **Evidence and Examples:** Add more specific examples and evidence to support the claims made about rats. Ensure that the evidence is relevant and effectively strengthens the argument.
3. **Counterarguments:** Address potential counterarguments to show a well-rounded understanding of the topic. This includes acknowledging differing viewpoints and then refuting them with evidence.
4. **Organization and Structure:** Revise the essay for a coherent structure. Each paragraph should focus on a specific point supporting the thesis. Use transition words to smoothly guide the reader from one point to the next.
5. **Conclusion:** Strengthen the conclusion by not only summarizing the main points but also by restating the importance of the argument and suggesting implications or actions that should be considered.
6. **Language and Style:** Pay attention to the choice of words and sentence structure. Aim for clear, concise language that maintains a formal tone appropriate for an argumentative essay.
7. **Proofreading:** Finally, proofread the essay for any grammatical or spelling errors. This will enhance the overall readability and professionalism of the piece.

Another way to train your AI partner to be a better coach is to *narrow the scope of feedback* you ask for. In this case, common sense will tell any writing teacher that the above list is too much feedback for one writer to take on at one time. It's also not very specific in its advice; it provides goals but not strategies or steps for achieving those goals. So make your prompt *more specific*. One way to do that is to focus your AI partner on one part of a writing task, such as the lead, structure, or transitions.

For instance, look at what happens when we revise our prompt to focus just on tips for improving the lead. We get back these suggestions:

 To improve the lead in alignment with the checklist, consider the following suggestions:

1. **Hook the Reader:** Start with an intriguing fact, question, or statement about rats that draws the reader in immediately. This could be a surprising statistic or a thought-provoking question.
2. **Introduce the Topic Clearly:** Briefly introduce what the essay is about. Make sure the reader understands that the essay will discuss rats, potentially focusing on a specific aspect such as their role in ecosystems, behavior, or common misconceptions.
3. **Thesis Statement:** Early in the introduction, clearly state your main argument or stance about rats. This thesis should guide the rest of the essay.
4. **Set the Tone:** Establish the tone of your essay in the lead. If your essay is persuasive, start with a confident tone; if it's informative, begin with a tone of curiosity or wonder.
5. **Engage with a Vivid Description:** If relevant, use a brief, vivid description or narrative about rats. This could be a personal anecdote or a general scenario that illustrates your main point.

You'll note how much more specific and helpful this feedback is. It includes strategies for how the writer might raise the level of their lead as well as goals.

It's also very helpful to find out what your AI partner would say if it weren't following your rubric or checklist, as a way to open yourself up to broader and unexpected feedback. Ask your AI partner about *beauties others might miss* in student writing. For instance, when we prompt our AI partner this way, we receive this:

One particularly unusual and impressive aspect of this 7th grader's writing that others might miss is their nuanced approach to cultural perspectives on rats. This demonstrates a level of cultural awareness and global thinking that is quite sophisticated for their age and the limited research time. Here are some key points that highlight this:

1. **Global Culinary Perspective:** The student doesn't just mention that rats are eaten, but provides specific examples from different cultures:
   - Chinese cuisine: They mention that rats are called "household deer" in China due to their taste resembling venison.
   - French haute cuisine: The essay notes that some high-end French restaurants serve rats that have been fed wine, highlighting a gourmet approach.
   - Mexican agricultural practice: The student points out that in Mexico, farmers eat the rats they catch in their crops.
2. **Scientific and Health Considerations:** The essay doesn't just state that rats are eaten, but also includes information about their nutritional value, mentioning protein and vitamin content. This shows an understanding of the intersection between cultural practices and scientific knowledge.
3. **Future-Oriented Thinking:** The student mentions that due to the large rat population, they could be a "future food source." This demonstrates an ability to connect current practices with potential future trends, which is an advanced cognitive skill.
4. **Non-Judgmental Presentation:** Despite the common Western aversion to eating rats, the student presents this information neutrally, without expressing disgust or judgment. This shows a remarkable level of cultural relativism and open-mindedness.
5. **Multifaceted View:** The essay presents rats not just as pests or pets (common Western views) but as food sources, research subjects, and resilient creatures. This multifaceted perspective is unusually comprehensive for a young writer.

> This global and culturally aware approach to the topic is quite rare for a 7th grade essay, especially one written in a single setting. It suggests a student who is not only curious about the world but also capable of synthesizing information from diverse sources to present a more complete picture of a topic. This kind of thinking is more commonly associated with much older students or even adults, making it a standout feature of this essay.

We love this. We would love to sit with this student right now and instead of talking only about his lead, talk about his *future-oriented thinking, nonjudgmental presentation,* and *global perspective*. This feedback illustrates why we've come to value AI as a writing coach. Sometimes it sees things we don't and says things we wouldn't. It opens up new possibilities.

Finally, let's think about Chavez's (2021) concerns with amplifying student voice and identity from *The Anti-Racist Writing Workshop*. We've already seen, with María's narrative, how you can train your AI partner to celebrate and cultivate students' cultural and linguistic capital. Another move you can make is to train your AI to be more responsive to students' quirky individuality. Take a moment to ask AI to *name something that feels unique and personal* about this student's writing. Then prompt your AI to respond to this aspect as an area of strength and potential growth. For instance, one thing that stands out is the writer's lively language. How could you not love the title "Rats and How They Roll?" It's quirky. It conveys a sense of the author's point of view: They are charmed by rats; they are rat defenders. It has a bit of an allusion and a bit of alliteration.

So let's revise our prompt to ask our AI partner to compliment this writer on his skill with language and suggest where in the piece he might build on those skills. Then our AI partner offers this feedback:

1. **Descriptive Imagery:** The essay includes descriptive imagery that helps to paint a clear and engaging picture of the subject. This makes the essay more lively and interesting to read.

2. **Use of Similes and Metaphors:** The writer effectively uses similes and metaphors, which add depth to the descriptions and help in drawing parallels that enhance understanding.
3. **Strong Vocabulary:** The use of a strong and varied vocabulary is evident, which is excellent for a 7th grade level. This enriches the essay and makes the argument more compelling.

Our AI partner also offers these tips, tailored to build from this writer's strengths:

1. **Consistent Use of Descriptive Language:** Encourage the writer to maintain the level of vivid description throughout the essay. This will help keep the reader engaged and strengthen the overall argument.
2. **Balancing Description with Argument:** While vivid language is powerful, it's important to balance it with clear, concise points that directly support the argument. Ensure that the descriptive language serves to enhance the argument, not overshadow it.
3. **Variety in Sentence Structure:** Experimenting with different sentence structures can add rhythm and interest to the writing. This variety can help maintain the reader's attention and emphasize key points.

You can see that training your AI partner to work from students' personal strengths will make your AI partner into a coach who augments your strengths, offering feedback you might not have considered.

A final tip for training your AI partner is to *ask it to provide examples*. Lots of students are mimetic writers who can mirror a pattern they see in demonstration writing. It's a lot to ask of teachers that they be highly proficient, fast drafters of elegant prose in any given moment. Yet students really need demonstration. If they knew *how* to write more powerfully, they would be doing it. When we prompt our AI partner to generate some examples of varied sentence structure, for example, it generates this:

 To add rhythm and interest through varied sentence structure in the essay about rats, consider the following example:

Original Sentence Structure:
"Rats are often misunderstood creatures. They are actually very clean and intelligent. Many people think they are dirty and carry diseases, but this is a misconception."

Revised for Varied Structure:
"Often misunderstood, rats are far more than what meets the eye. Contrary to popular belief, these creatures exhibit a high level of cleanliness and intelligence, debunking the myth of them being mere disease carriers."

In this revision, the structure starts with an introductory clause ("Often misunderstood"), followed by a contrasting statement ("Contrary to popular belief"). This not only adds variety to the sentence structure but also emphasizes the point more effectively, creating a more engaging and rhythmic flow in the writing.

That's a pretty helpful tool for sitting next to a student and teaching about varied sentence structure. You might only share the example, or you might name these new parts (introductory clauses, contrasting statements). Either way, you have an example in seconds that you can share with a student. You could also further tailor this prompt by telling your AI partner about writers this student admires and giving it a sample, so that its examples reflect that style.

You'll notice that we're not prompting AI to compose large swaths of writing or to generate drafts. Instead, we're using AI to hone student voice, celebrate student voice, develop student purpose, and build on student strengths.

Model the writing behaviors that you want to instill in your students by showing them how to use AI as a partner and coach, not a substitute. Foster a sense of pride in their own voice and agency so that they see AI as one of the tools in their toolkit. You can train your AI partner to be a better writing coach by

- Providing it with tools such as checklists, rubrics, or learning goals.
- Narrowing the scope of feedback; be specific about the part of writing to focus on.
- Teaching it to celebrate students' cultural and linguistic capital.
- Asking it to see and name beauties others might miss, respecting its wider vision and ability to see the unexpected.
- Asking for strategies as well as goals.
- Leading it to focus on student strengths and individual language.
- Inviting it to provide examples of demonstration writing.
- Providing it with mentor texts that students want to emulate.

Remember, you can mediate all the feedback that AI provides. Your AI partner will give you a deep toolbox of possible feedback, and you can make choices from this feedback. The joy is that the toolbox is refilled instantly, it communicates in many languages, and it extends your own repertoire.

Visit ai-enhancedliteracy.org if you'd like some practical support with uploading rubrics to AI, asking it to analyze mentor texts, or honing prompts across a chat.

Setting Up Edtech Chats for Student Writers

Everything you learn by studying AI feedback and experimenting with coaching your AI partner, as you play with ChatGPT or Claude or the open AI of your choice, will help you as you set up edtech chat rooms for student writers. Your edtech platform will allow you to shape how your students interact with AI, which gives them a lot of training that will help them when they continue these interactions independently. You can also put up guardrails that prevent students from using AI to avoid writing themselves—an ethical trap and, perhaps even worse, a path that will prevent students from building the writing skills they'll need in high-stakes assessments and other situations where they can't use AI. We especially love edtech AI platforms like Flint that allow teachers to be specific in how they want their AI partner to interact with student writers.

Teach Your Edtech AI to Insist Students Come with Work in Hand

Give your edtech AI partner very specific direction on how to launch their chat with students, including how to insist that students come to their AI partner with some work in hand. For instance, you might prompt the following:

> Act as a thought partner to my 7th graders as they come up with ideas for their memoirs. Insist that they tell you at least five things about themselves before you share some story ideas, so that these ideas are personal to each student. If students need support sharing information, suggest they share information about the books, movies, and shows they love, how they spend their time outside school, and what worries and preoccupies them. Give your story ideas as possible titles or themes. Do not write any of these stories for students.

If your students are writing literary essays, tell your edtech AI that students must share some of their notes and thinking before asking for help. For instance, you might prompt the following:

> My 9th graders are getting ready to write literary essays on *The Catcher in the Rye* by J. D. Salinger. They have annotated the text and have notes. Invite students to share their ideas so far, including possible themes, ideas about characters, literary techniques they noticed, and parts of the text they found intriguing. Support them in developing three to four possible topics or theses, based on what they've each found interesting in the book so far. Do not write any part of their essay for them—be a discussion partner.

Instruct Your Edtech Partner to Ask How Much (and What Kind of) Feedback Writers Want

Edtech AI, like all AI, can generate heaps of feedback. You can set up your edtech AI to give three compliments and three possible next steps for a writer when they share their drafts. Or you can prompt it to ask writers, "How much feedback would you like? Would you like feedback just on your introduction or the whole piece? Would you like feedback on one aspect of the rubric?" It's good for students to learn that AI can overwhelm the writer, so they need to tell their AI partner how much feedback they want.

Encourage Your Edtech AI to Coach the Writer, Not Fix the Piece

Kids will seek a lot of support from their AI partner, and it can give them too much support unless you set boundaries. Tell your edtech AI partner that you want your students to become stronger writers and that the goal is more important than the piece they are currently writing. Explain that you want the feedback writers get to help them imagine how to put that feedback into play in this piece and be transferable to the next. You might instruct your edtech AI to give students feedback on how they respond to feedback, across multiple drafts.

Ensure Your Edtech AI Coaches Within Ethical Boundaries

Your edtech AI can not only make suggestions but also draft swaths or whole pieces of writing. That's both unethical and bad for students' development. You might want to read Ethan Mollick's (2025) blog post "Post-Apocalyptic Education." In it, he shares how flawed AI detectors are, in both purpose and effectiveness. Instead of turning to detectors, he suggests really working with students to understand how the goal of homework is to build skills for students to then use in high-stakes moments and endeavors. Then you can explain that you will say explicitly to your edtech AI that you do not want it to write for students—because you care about them. Sometimes that directive of "never" is too draconian, as it can help students to see snippets or examples of what a writing technique might look like. So you could also say, "Never write more than two sentences for a student, and always do so as part of showing a few choices or examples with explanation." The main thing is to insist on and explain ethical boundaries.

AI as an Instructional Planning Partner

Your AI partner should not only expand the range of feedback possibilities you can offer students but also help you with being able to reach more students in less time, with more precision. The impossibility of giving feedback in a timely enough fashion so that students still care about it and can use it is something that haunts all writing teachers. Here are a few different ways you can turn your AI partner into an instructional planner.

Planning Whole-Group Lessons (Genre Knowledge and Data)

There are two main ways to use AI to plan whole-group lessons. The first is by leaning on genre knowledge, and the second is by leaning on assessment data.

To lean on genre knowledge, decide what genre you want to teach your students to become more powerful at, and ask your AI partner to list possible teaching points. As long as you are teaching a common genre such as argument essays or narratives, your AI partner will provide a collection of possible instruction. We also find that we get good results when we ask our AI partner, "What are 10 qualities of powerful…?" For instance, when we ask for qualities of powerful arguments, we get this list:

Here are 10 qualities of powerful written arguments:

1. Clear thesis: A strong, specific claim that clearly states the argument's position.
2. Logical structure: A well-organized flow of ideas that builds the arguments systematically.
3. Solid evidence: Relevant, credible facts, statistics, and expert opinions that support the main claim.
4. Sound reasoning: Logical connections between evidence and conclusions, avoiding fallacies.
5. Balanced perspective: Acknowledgment and refutation of counterarguments to strengthen credibility.
6. Persuasive language: Effective uses of rhetorical devices and tone appropriate to the audience.

> 7. Coherence: Smooth transitions and connections between ideas and paragraphs.
> 8. Credible sources: Use of reliable, authoritative references to bolster the argument.
> 9. Engaging introduction: An opening that captures attention and establishes the argument's importance.
> 10. Compelling conclusion: A strong ending that reinforces the main points and leaves a lasting impression.

We can easily imagine turning this list into teaching points for argument writing. And remember, you can then ask your AI partner to help draft demonstration writing for these qualities.

To lean on assessment data, gather some student drafts. You might give an on-demand assessment, asking students to draft a quick two-page argument on a topic they care about. Or you can ask students to flash draft early in the writing process. Gather these drafts, and choose four or five pieces that represent a lot of your writers. Invite your AI partner to analyze this collection and generate teaching suggestions and potential feedback. This will help you tailor your teaching approach to the specific needs of the students in front of you. We've found that our AI partners tend to do a better job when they analyze 5 pieces than when they analyze 30. The feedback is more specific. Choosing a few prototypical pieces will give your AI partner enough information for it to help you shape your instruction. You can also study the reports that your edtech AI gives you, if you set up edtech chats for students to seek writing feedback.

Planning Targeted Small Groups, Conferences, and Intervention

Gather your student data. It might be observational and relational. For instance, you may have gathered observations about which students write more powerfully in languages other than English, or you may have noticed which students would benefit from speech-to-text software or which would love a starter list of possible ideas for topics. Or your data might be gathered from early drafts, which will give you information about students' control of structure, craft, focus, and conventions. Either way, if you sort your students into groupings, you can then turn to your AI partner to help create targeted instruction and tools for these groups. Figure 3.3 includes some suggestions.

Figure 3.3
Using AI to Support Responsive Instruction

If...	Then...
Students can write in more than one language	Use AI to translate student work so that you (and they) can see and respond to their full competencies as writers
Students would benefit from hearing feedback in more than one language	Use AI to translate your feedback (speech or text) to increase and humanize communication
Students say more than they write	Set students up with an AI-powered writing assistant (such as Grammarly) to capture their words in print
Students write at different proficiency levels	Ask AI to generate different levels of demonstration texts
Students would like support with coming up with ideas	Use AI to generate a list of possible topics, themes, or ideas as a starter set for students
Students would like support with structure	Ask AI to analyze a mentor text for parts so that students can write within these parts
Students want to explore craft	Ask AI to analyze mentor texts or student writing for particularly effective craft
Students want support with conventions	Ask AI to act as an editor—and ask it to explain its suggestions

Planning Communication About Writing Skills with Students and Families

Any teacher (or school leader) who has written observations and narratives to communicate with students and families knows that this is a significant and daunting task. For secondary teachers, it's not unusual to have over a hundred of these short narratives. It's reasonable, then, to consider if AI can help educators with this task. Of course, nothing replaces your human knowledge of students—what you know about their work habits, their classroom interactions, their wit and warmth and quirks. Imagine, though, if your AI partner could study the most recent piece of writing of each student and in seconds generate a list of qualities that writing demonstrates as well as a short list of possible next steps for them as writers. You could then add on your personal knowledge of the child. If you set students up with edtech AI, they can each get personalized feedback as soon as they write—and then you can talk to kids about that feedback, maximizing your personal interactions.

We've found this merging of AI writing expertise and speed with teacher knowledge creates productive and efficient communication. It blends teacher knowledge with analysis of student writing, and it takes a herculean task and makes it manageable. And of course, you can also use your AI partner to translate these communications. We do advocate for transparency. Let your community know that the school turns to an AI partner to help assess student writing and to translate communications. Knowing that teachers are technologically adept as well as in close relationships with students should serve you well.

Teaching Kids Wise Ways as Digital Writers

All the AI-generated writing support that we've laid out here that teachers can do—to get help with idea-building, to seek feedback, to ask for demonstration writing—is also at your students' fingertips. Whereas 10 years ago, the biggest help students might seek were spell-checks and grammar checks, now AI can write a lively personal narrative, a well-reasoned argument, or evocative poetry.

Our biggest tip is, don't wallow in nostalgia. There was never a time in the past when all our students strove at writing, put in many hours at improving a piece, sought personal feedback, and met their deadlines with grace. The kinds of writing kids do for school have always been easier for some students than for others. Students have always worried that their own writing wasn't strong enough and sought support in a lot of ways, some wise and some less so. Writing has always been a learnable craft that, like any craft, takes practice. None of that has changed. What has changed is the repertoire of support available for writers.

Your first task, then, will be to teach your students about the writing and learning process and help them believe that it is worth it to work on their writing. Assure them that they can become more powerful writers and that this skill will help them think more clearly, communicate more fluently, and read more attentively. Let them know that AI can, in fact, be a tremendous help. But your goal is for them to learn how to use AI wisely so that they work within ethical boundaries, improve their own skills while getting support, and become as fluent as possible.

It helps to think about assessment. A lot of high-stakes assessments, like IB and AP assessments, are essentially on-demand writing tasks, written in one sitting, without the benefit of AI. For students who value performance on these assessments, you can point to these experiences and create similar writing experiences to help students get better at this kind of on-demand writing. With these kinds of assessments, students' interactions with AI can serve as a form of skill development during preparation or self-assessment after they have written, or they can create learning goals from the feedback AI regularly gives on their on-demand writing.

You also want to teach students the value of working at a piece over time and how to use all the tools available to become a stronger writer and to improve a piece. Note that these last two are not interchangeable. It's much easier to fix up a piece than it is to improve as a writer. One is fast; one takes practice. To improve a piece, you can teach students how to seek AI feedback, add that feedback into their writing, and use AI to support conventions. To improve as a writer, you can teach them the value of mentor texts, planning with structure in mind, studying writing craft, redrafting in response to feedback, learning from convention suggestions, and striving to develop your own voice and purpose.

You can also value process over product in your assessment process and shift your assessments so that writing is more generative and less high stakes. Rather than focusing solely on the final product, shift toward valuing the writing process itself by embracing assessment methods that celebrate the revision, both big and small, along the way. This approach recognizes that incremental improvement is an iterative process, demanding that we circle back, challenge our initial thoughts, and explore new angles. One-and-done writing often centers the quality of initial performance, whereas experienced writers and learners develop from taking risks, learning from missteps, and gradually refining their craft over time.

Figure 3.4 includes some of the teaching points we suggest when teaching young writers about interacting with AI as a writing coach.

Figure 3.4
Teaching Points for Coaching Writers Alongside AI

Writing Stage	Teaching Point
Collecting and generating ideas	• Writers often find it helpful to tell AI about their interests and then preview AI-suggested personal themes or topics to find new ideas to explore in their writing. • Writers should consider their own passions, interests, experience, and vision as they choose what to write about. • Writers can turn to AI to summarize their research notes to highlight main points and potential themes.
Drafting	• Writers can ask AI to break a mentor text into parts to help plan a draft. • Writers can ask AI for the main qualities of a genre so that they have these in mind as they write. • Writers can ask AI to create an outline from their notes to help them imagine structure for a draft. • Writers should be wary of asking AI to generate writing, as writers will lose their voice and perspective, miss the opportunity to learn and grow, and stray into unethical terrain.
Revising	• Once they've drafted, writers can seek specific feedback from AI on their structure, craft, or conventions. • Once they've drafted, writers can seek feedback on parts of their writing from AI, such as their introduction or conclusion. • Writers will accept some AI feedback and reject some, as they consider their vision, purpose, and voice. • Writers can give their AI partner feedback, telling it what they don't want to change, advising it on their own goals. • Writers can ask AI to use a rubric or checklist to provide class-normed feedback on their draft and suggest next steps. • Writers can train their AI partner to make suggestions that sustain their voice by uploading prior writing samples as mentor texts.
Publishing	• Writers can ask an AI assistant to prepare their resources as an accurate bibliography. • Writers can turn to AI for support with editing for conventions. • Writers may acknowledge AI support with a footnote or author's note, following community norms (e.g., "I used Zotero to generate my bibliography"; "I sought feedback from ChatGPT while drafting"; "I used Grammarly to support my editing process").

Share Your Own Writing Process and Interactions with AI

One of the most powerful methods for instilling wise ways in your students is to share your own process. When students see how AI can be helpful to you as a writer and how, without care, it can submerge your writer's voice and intention, they'll be better prepared (and will believe in) this process for themselves. Your AI partner will be in a dialogue with you—and the naturalness (and sometimes annoying aspects) of it make the process pleasantly motivating (Mollick & Mollick, 2023).

Here's an example, for instance, of Phil sharing his writing and interactions with his AI coach with students. He starts with a snippet of his own writing, modeling how he comes to AI having already done a little generating, seeking feedback.

This is a sample from a story I wrote that I often share with students. It showcases a writing move I want them to learn. If I was a student, in middle school, what advice would you give me:

My saxophone case banged against the doorframe as I shuffled into my house. My dad sat up on the couch. I clearly woke him up from a nap. Dark circles surrounded his eyes. It seemed like he was always working the night shift now.

"I have to come clean," I thought to myself. "No way can I tell him, not today," I continued to ruminate over my decision.

I was thinking that it was time to come clean. I had just dropped out of the band.

Instead, I smiled at my dad and I started to walk to my room not saying a word.

But my dad sat up and said, "how's the music lessons going?"

I hesitated. Sweat stared to bead on my forehead. "Great," I said. "My teacher says I have lots of potential."

"That's wonderful. I'm so proud of you."

Next, Phil shares what AI suggested to him as a writer:

Firstly, kudos on the writing sample! It's engaging and paints a vivid picture for readers. Here's feedback tailored for a middle school student:

Strengths:

1. **Descriptive Details:** The way you described the protagonist's entrance and the father's appearance gives the reader a clear image. Descriptions like "My saxophone case banged against the door frame" and "Dark circles surrounded his eyes" are evocative and set the scene well.
2. **Internal Conflict:** The protagonist's inner dialogue ("I have to come clean..." captures their inner turmoil effectively, allowing readers to empathize with their dilemma.
3. **Show, Don't Tell:** Instead of directly saying the protagonist was nervous, you conveyed it through their actions and feelings: "Sweat started to bead on my forehead."

Phil can share how AI surprises him with its insights. For instance, he himself hadn't recognized that "coming clean" was the central moment of internal conflict. Now he can look across the rest of his story and see if he really developed this conflict across the beginning, middle, and end or if it only exists in this one part. Maybe he can chat with AI a little more about that.

Phil can also model how he considers feedback on next steps from his AI coach, accepting some of it and rejecting some of it. He models that AI is a coach, not a replacement for the writer.

Suggestions for Improvement:

1. **Avoid Repetition:** You've mentioned the thought of "coming clean" a few times. It might be more effective to condense this. For example, "I hesitated, thoughts of coming clean about dropping out of the band racing through my mind. But, faced with my dad's hopeful expression, I just couldn't."

> 2. **Dialogue Flow:** When characters speak, try to ensure their dialogue flows naturally. For instance, instead of "how's the music lessons going?" consider "How are your music lessons going?"
> 3. **Use Varied Sentence Structures:** Mixing up short and long sentences can make the narrative more dynamic. For instance, instead of "I smiled at my dad and I started to walk to my room not saying a word," you might try: "I smiled at my dad and started to walk to my room, silent."

Phil might decide to accept the critique of repetition, or he might decide his repetition is deliberate. This could be a moment to have students discuss what they would do with the feedback. Ask if they agree. Ultimately, you're looking to show students that you'll accept some feedback and reject other feedback.

In this piece, Phil can also reject the correction to his father's dialogue. He can note that his AI partner doesn't know how his father speaks, and the suggestions would make the character feel less realistic. Phil can not only reject that feedback but also make sure he tells his AI partner that he wants his characters to sound realistic so that it doesn't give him more feedback like this later in the conversation. Say, "I'm going to give my AI partner some feedback!"

Critiquing AI feedback is a powerful way to get students to think more critically about feedback that they receive in general and to become more thoughtful of what they are producing. This process counteracts AI as a tool that flattens creativity and individuality and positions it so it can support the creativity and brilliance students bring to our classrooms each and every day.

Embracing AI as Part of the Future of Writing

AI is most immediately, visibly useful as a partner in the writing process. For writers, it can help them generate ideas, raise the level of their writing, and get it ready for publication. For teachers, it can help them celebrate writers' progress, select and communicate feedback, study trends, plan curriculum, and tailor instruction and assessments. AI is both a huge time saver and an expert instructor. It can be bossy and overwhelming and didactic, like any instructor. It can over-scaffold, like any teacher. The one thing it's not going to do is go away. We have a moral imperative to teach young people how to use AI wisely and ethically so that they learn from it how to be more powerful, original writers. We have a personal need to teach ourselves how to use it wisely and efficiently so that we free more of our hearts and souls to give to our students, our families, and the world around us.

Deepening Reading Comprehension with Digital Texts and Tools

Earlier in our teaching careers, parents and caregivers would ask us, Does it matter if my child is mostly reading digitally? We would tend to say that the platform didn't matter. What mattered was that the child was falling in love with reading. To a certain extent, that is still true. A lot of avid readers, ourselves included, read on Kindles and other digital platforms. When you read a lot, you appreciate the instant access to books and the ability to carry them with you everywhere you go. A lot of avid readers, ourselves included, also listen to audiobooks and nonfiction podcasts as a huge part of their reading lives. When you drive a lot, exercise, or are engaged in otherwise tedious tasks, podcasts and audiobooks are marvelous.

What we didn't realize until more recent research emerged—and we had more years observing young people's shifting reading habits in classrooms—was that there is a difference between engagement and adeptness. Digital texts are more engaging. There is a reason that the *New York Times* is getting so many awards for its digital journalism, with its gorgeous maps and charts and embedded videos. But it is also harder to read digitally with high comprehension. The distractors are greater, but there is also something else: It is harder to deploy your greatest superpowers as readers.

In this chapter, we'll consider the following:

- The superpowers of reading.
- What happens when we read digitally.
- Creating tools and edtech spaces to support students who read below benchmark.
- Accepting a digital future for reading.

The Superpowers of Reading

When we think about what makes reading work—what transforms marks on a page or screen into understanding, emotion, and insight—we find that successful readers consistently draw upon three essential superpowers. These abilities aren't mysterious or innate; they're skills that can be taught, practiced, and strengthened over time. As we move deeper into digital reading environments, especially AI-enhanced reading environments, we understand these core superpowers of previewing, rereading, and focus become increasingly vital for teachers and students alike.

Previewing Is a Superpower

The first of these essential reading superpowers is *previewing* a text. When you preview a text, looking at the back cover of the novel, for instance, or scanning down a nonfiction text, noting the subheadings, the images, the parts, you start your reading at a higher level. Your brain already knows what to expect and is ready to attach new information to this structure. If, for instance, young readers pick up the young adult novel *How Tía Lola Came to Visit Stay*, by Julia Alvarez, and read the back blurb, they'll see and read:

> When Miguel's Tía Lola comes from the Dominican Republic to Vermont to help out his mami, Miguel is worried that his unusual aunt will make it even more difficult to make new friends. It's been hard enough moving from New York City and leaving Papi behind. Sometimes he wishes Tía Lola would go back to the island.
>
> But then he wouldn't have the treats she's putting in his lunch box, which he's sure helped him make the baseball team. And she really needs his help to learn English so she doesn't use all the words she knows at once: "One-way-caution-you're-welcome-thanks-for-asking."
>
> So Miguel changes his wish to a new one, and he finally even figures out a clever way to make it come true.

There is so much information here. Before opening the first page of the book, the young reader knows that the main character's name is Miguel who has recently moved from New York City to Vermont. They know about Miguel's joys and sadness: that his Papi didn't come with them and that he wants to make the baseball team. They know that the central issue in the story (on top of these other challenges Miguel faces) is the arrival of Miguel's aunt, Tía Lola, from the Dominican Republic. They know Miguel is a little insecure and is worried that Tía Lola won't fit in, that she doesn't speak English fluently, and that she needs help communicating. From the cover, they can see that Tía Lola wears bright island colors in this cold snowy landscape. Visit ai-enhanced literacy.org to see the full cover.

Now when readers begin to read, they expect to meet Miguel. They are not surprised when the first page tells them Tía Lola arrives tomorrow. They are already aware of Miguel's emotional state and can look for clues that give them extra insight. They start reading already knowledgeable about the main character, the setting, and the central conflicts.

Now let's imagine teen readers, researching the oceans and environmental changes, as they prepare to read *World Without Fish*, written by Mark Kurlansky and illustrated by Frank Stockton. Visit ai-enhancedliteracy.org to see the full cover. As they scan the covers, they'll see and read:

> Can you imagine a world without fish? It's not as crazy as it sounds. But if we keep doing things the way we've been doing things, fish could become extinct within fifty years. So let's change the way we do things!

Again, there is some crucial information. In "Effective Practices for Developing Reading Comprehension," Nell K. Duke and P. David Pearson note that "good readers typically *look over* the text before they read, noting such things as the *structure* of the text and text sections that might be most relevant to their reading goals" (2009, p. 107). When they preview, these young readers will learn that this book asks how we could let a world without fish happen—and that this is a real environmental possibility. They'll also learn that there are keys to solving this crisis. As they flip through the pages before reading, they'll learn that Mark Kurlansky was a commercial fisherman before he became an advocate for the oceans. They'll see that the book has a hybrid structure and will teach them in a few different ways: Some parts are narrative nonfiction, including graphic novel parts. Some parts are expository. In all parts, the graphics and images give additional information. They'll see that the book ends with resources both for more learning and for taking action. All of this information lets young readers make a plan for reading, taking notes, and talking about the book as they read.

Rereading Is a Superpower

A second superpower for readers is *rereading*. Teachers have known forever how much repeated reading increases comprehension. In 1989, in her article in *The Reading Teacher* entitled "Repeated Reading: Research into Practice," Sarah L. Dowhower shared multiple studies showing that rereading dramatically increases comprehension. More recently, Nell K. Duke and Kelly B. Cartwright (2021), in "The Science of Reading Progresses: Communicating Advances Beyond the Simple View of Reading," suggest that active self-regulation is one of three key components of reading success derived from reading research. Active readers monitor their comprehension and reread on the run as they make meaning. It's a rapid, automatic process that deepens comprehension.

We'll never forget visiting colleagues at Educational Testing Service, in the department named CBAL (Cognitively Based Assessment of, for, and as Learning), and seeing some of the results of eye-tracking assessments. When you looked at the patterns of less successful readers who remembered less and demonstrated partial comprehension, you would often see in fiction a diligent left to right pattern, moving across each line, always moving forward. With nonfiction, you would see big spaces where the eye pattern skipped over hard parts. When you looked at the patterns of successful readers who remembered what they read and demonstrated high comprehension, the pattern in fiction generally was one that moved down the middle of the page, with a lot of revisiting of the text, and in nonfiction there was a lot of lingering in hard parts, rereading several times.

There are a lot of research studies showing correlation between "eye-gaze analysis" and reading comprehension (Berzak et al., 2018; Lima Sanches et al., 2018; Mézière et al., 2023). Mézière and colleagues (2023) in particular describe *saccades* (rapid, ballistic eye movements), *fixations* (pauses when the eyes are stationary), and *regressions* (where eyes move back to an earlier part of the text).

Think of your own reading experiences when you are reading print. Chances are, when you find the novel confusing, you flip back a few pages. When you pick up your book after putting it down, you'll often go back to a bit before you started. When the article you're reading has dense information or complicated charts or fascinating maps, you'll pore over those parts. You are rereading all the time. If you were hooked up to an eye-tracking machine, you would see not only saccades but also fixations and regressions on parts of the text, as you worked to make meaning. Louise M. Rosenblatt (1982) taught that reading is transactional, meaning happens between the text and the reader, and each reader evokes distinct meaning in this transaction. Rosenblatt brought an awareness of the text of the self that is involved in reading, the way we bring our experiences, perspectives, longings, interests, and biases to what we read. Reading is also transactional in that it doesn't happen without the reader *working at it*.

In *Reader, Come Home*, Maryanne Wolf (2018) reminds us that we were never meant to read, as in, we don't have a genetic program for reading like language, vision, and cognitive processes. Reading is a cultural invention. As we learn to read and work at reading, our brain develops new synapses. We'll return to this idea in a moment. For now, think about how each time you pause and decide "I should go back," you are making an important reading decision. And print is easy to reread. After a while, powerful readers barely notice that they reread, because it is an automatic process.

Focus Is a Superpower

The third superpower, alongside previewing and rereading, is the ability to *focus*. Really focusing, engaging in what Maryanne Wolf (2018) calls *deep reading* processes, is essential not only for reading comprehension but also for reading to be pleasurable. Wolf describes how, when you read, your brain is building synapses for critical analysis and empathy. We love the idea that your brain literally grows and changes—that you become a different kind of person— because you read. Wolf notes, though, how this kind of deep, immersive reading, where you are lost in a story or captivated by an article, requires allocation of time and cognitive patience. In *Stolen Focus*, reading scholar Raymond Mar explains to Johann Hari that "while we're reading, we're directing attention outward toward the words on the page and, at the same time, enormous amounts of attention is going inward as we imagine and mentally simulate" (Hari, 2022, pp. 87–88).

Hari devotes a whole chapter in *Stolen Focus* to the concept of *flow states*, a term first described by the psychologist Mihaly Csikszentmihalyi (2022) as "the deepest form of focus and attention that we know of" (p. 55). Deep reading in that on average provides the lowest amount of flow" (Hari, 2022, p. 59). And once a reader is interrupted and not comprehending all that well, then reading becomes harder and less pleasurable. Then you do it less, and you stop liking it, and you become the young person who says, "I don't like reading," when what they mean is "I find reading hard."

You can mull over, as we often do, some of the challenges and beauties of digital texts, here in Figure 4.1.

Figure 4.1
The Beauty and Challenge of Digital Texts

Beauties	Challenges
• There is instant access to engaging texts. • There are embedded images, graphics, and videos. • There are flexible font sizes and layout to increase readability. • There is instant access to glossaries, Wikipedia information, and related links. • You have the ability to listen to fantastic readers. • The device is portable, and you can carry many texts, wherever you go. • The device often serves as a reading log or reservoir of reading.	• Previewing is inconvenient, challenging, or impossible. • Rereading is inconvenient, both as an on-the-run process and for large chunks of text. • Lower comprehension related to lack of previewing and rereading decrease focus and flow state. • Distractors in the text (hyperlinks, ads) and via the media of a smart device interrupt focus and flow state. • It's considerably harder to achieve deep reading and deep comprehension.

Increasing Digital Comprehension: Deepening Strategies and Habits

It's a tricky conundrum for teachers, knowing that their students are going to do almost everything digitally, including reading, while also realizing that their understanding and concentration are going to be compromised in this media. Students will also be vulnerable to distractors when reading digitally, as well as the inflammatory aspects of all social media.

It's on teachers, then, to make sure you are teaching students about the joys and pitfalls of digital texts, as well as how to develop some thoughtful strategies

It's a little different with nonfiction. Previewing a nonfiction text helps readers understand its essential structure. As you get to know the parts of the upcoming text, you also become familiar with what it is going to teach you, how the content is divided into parts, and what features and formatting stand out. You can do that work with a digital text, but it's just hard enough that you don't. You'd have to scroll all the way down before reading or scroll across a video to see how long it is. It's worth it, but digital readers rarely do that work unless someone teaches them its importance.

The same is true of rereading. In his 2022 interview with Wolf, Ezra Klein said of rereading with digital texts, "You can go back. But you never do. And so things go missing. And the things that go missing may in some instances be the most important facts or details to understanding the plot or understanding the argument." Think of your own experience with audiobooks, podcasts, online articles, even your ebook. It's not that you couldn't find the pause button and rewind, replay, or scroll back. It's just inconvenient enough that you don't do it. This failure to reread may also be related to the fact that often, digital readers are multitasking. They listen while they drive, making it not only inconvenient but unsafe to replay something. They're exercising or doing dishes, meaning they also have lower expectations for their comprehension. They become accustomed to the text flowing over them.

That experience of text washing over us is *not a flow state*. It's not focus; in fact, it is somewhat the opposite of it. Two troubles arise with this kind of low-level attention. One is that the reader becomes accustomed to not focusing, to not expecting to fully grasp the text because it's inconvenient or impossible to preview and reread. Another is that the reader is then open to distractors, of which there may be many, both inside and around the digital text. Simply because the delivery service is a smart device, messages are popping up, other apps are asking for your attention, and the text itself may include links that lead the reader out of the text and into another text, advertisements, or other digital spaces.

In *The Shallows: What the Internet Is Doing to Our Brains,* Nicholas Carr (2011) speaks of how novelty bias makes us susceptible to the false, the fake, misinformation, missing details, and missing sequence because it is all packaged so glibly and attractively. If we were focusing and rereading, we would be less susceptible to novelty bias. The same researcher who studied flow states, Csikszentmihalyi, described to Hari how fragile and easily disrupted flow states are. He warns that "staring at a screen is one of the activities we take part shows similar results. Digital reading poses more challenges to comprehension than print. Ferris Jabr (2013) describes how "whether they realize it or not, many people approach computers and tablets with a state of mind less conducive to learning than the one they bring to paper" (para. 6).

Nevertheless, we embrace digital reading, while knowing full well that it is fraught with difficulties. We don't want it to stop or want to prevent it from happening in school, because we know that young people mostly read digitally. We think all teachers need to teach into it. Teachers need to do their very best to ensure that deep reading habits are inculcated as early as possible, and they need to acknowledge the particular challenges that arise when reading digitally and teach strategies to respond to these challenges.

Challenges to Comprehension with Digital Reading

Let's look first at the challenges that are embedded in digital reading, by returning to these three reading superpowers: *previewing, rereading,* and *focus.* All of these are harder when you are reading an ebook or listening to a podcast or an audiobook. Previewing is essentially impossible. If you have 40 minutes, listen to Wolf's interview, "The Future of the Reading Brain in an Increasingly Digital World" (Chakrabarti, 2018). In it, she discusses *haptic dissonance,* which happens when your brain can no longer picture an object with any solidity. To grasp this concept, think about a book that you remember from childhood. It might be one someone read to you or one you read yourself. We picture *Charlotte's Web, The Chronicles of Narnia, The Very Hungry Caterpillar,* and *The Hardy Boys.* Ask your colleagues to do the same. Almost everyone can picture not only the cover but also the pages, the font, and what the book looks and feels like. It turns out that part of how you remember text is you remember it physically, even to what the words look like on the page. Now picture that same text as an ebook. *Charlotte's Web* and *Things Fall Apart* look the same. They both have the same page layout and font size that we've chosen as readers. You can't tell how long the book is, how many pages are left, or where you are in the chapter. That's haptic dissonance. Your brain has no tangible anchors for locating where you are in a text or remembering it.

We recognize this experience. We are both avid readers, and we now read a lot on Kindles. We often fail to remember the title of a book now when we want to recommend it to a friend. We are surprised to find ourselves in the last chapter. We remember covers of books we read as children, with all the information included there, better than those we read last week.

is a classic flow state. The reader becomes absorbed by the text. Their imagination, heart, and mind are all entangled in the words they read and the images, thoughts, and feelings they provoke. When reading is successful, it is magical. That's why successful readers become avid readers. When teachers encourage independent reading and reading for pleasure, it's not because they value fun, as some think. It's because when reading is working, it is pleasurable and something you do by choice. Because you read a lot, your brain grows, you learn more, and your analytic skills and empathy expand.

It's helpful to think about when you enter flow states. For some, it's when climbing, running, or dancing. For others, it might be playing guitar or painting. Athletics and artistic endeavors tend to induce flow states. But mathematicians enter flow states, as do physicists and writers. Think about those moments when you are utterly concentrated, completely engaged in an experience. That's what you want reading to be like for your students. Csikszentmihalyi says, "One of the simplest and most common forms of flow that people experience in their lives is reading a book" (Hari, 2022, p. 55).

What Happens When We Read Digitally

There are great advantages to digital reading, including the following:

- Instant access to texts.
- Embedded images and graphics and links.
- The ability to increase font size to make it easier to read.
- The ability to look up words and phrases as you read.
- The ability to have things read to you by fantastic readers.
- The ability to carry with you so very many texts, wherever you go.

These are huge advantages, which is why so many of us now read digitally, almost exclusively. Ask your colleagues, and you'll find that many are devoted to podcasts, audiobooks, or ebooks. And it is beautiful that reading has expanded in all these ways. The world is a multimodal place, and digital platforms make reading more available and more engaging—it's a more democratic experience.

It's also a reading experience that rarely induces high comprehension. In *How We Read Now*, Naomi S. Baron (2022) explains that there are important differences in the way we concentrate, understand, and remember across multiple formats. She warns of the hazards of digital reading for critical thinking. Her research demonstrates that heavy readers of social media have lower reading comprehension scores. Wolf's (2018) research in *Reader, Come Home* and habits. We encourage you to have a round of podcast clubs or audiobook clubs to help students practice taking notes from digital texts, rereading digital texts, and learning to focus with them. We encourage you to demonstrate reading digital nonfiction, so that together you can navigate the text features and hyperlinks and study how the ads are designed to either mimic the text or entice the individual reader by their online profile. It's important to practice this work in school, thinking about what's tricky and being transparent with young people so that they can become adept and powerful readers.

To figure out what to teach, we ask ourselves, What's particularly challenging here? What can we do in response? For instance, knowing that readers will miss out on all the information available on the back cover of novels that sets them up to start their reading at a higher level, you can teach students to seek book reviews that will similarly introduce the text. You can show them how to access author websites, how to find descriptions on Goodreads, and how to find interviews with the author on YouTube. Knowing that previewing digital nonfiction is also challenging, you can add that into your own read-aloud or text introductions, making it a typical experience to collaboratively preview a text before getting started.

Wolf's research suggests that students can develop multiple reading styles so that they bring their best reading selves to different modalities of texts. She talks about the bilateral brain, suggesting that students can learn print strategies and deep reading processes while they also learn coding and cognitive processes that go with digital reading (Klein, 2022; Wolf, 2018).

This is new terrain for a lot of classrooms, although it can initially feel like old terrain. Often, we see digital texts, including in primary grades, where students read on platforms like Epic, and in upper grades, where high-stakes assessments are often digital now. But it's still less common to see attention to strategy instruction to support digital reading. That's probably because we assume engagement will lead to comprehension. It can also be because we assume students don't need this kind of instruction anymore. After all, they learned to preview texts in 1st grade. But everything changes when the texts become digital, and it's worth teaching these strategies, with fresh demonstrations, in complex digital texts.

Figure 4.2 includes the most effective instructional moves we've found for deepening digital reading comprehension.

Figure 4.2
Strategies to Deepen Digital Comprehension

When getting ready to read digital narratives, readers *find out a bit about the story*, such as the main character, where the story takes place, some of the big conflicts. Without back covers, they do this by
- Reading online reviews.
- Reading a Goodreads or Amazon description.
- Visiting the author's website.
- Finding interviews with the author.

When starting digital narratives, readers *take a moment to orient themselves*. They do this by studying
- The table of contents.
- The overall length.
- What tools are available, including how to reread, how to look up vocabulary, how to annotate, and how to note your location in the text.

When getting ready to read nonfiction, readers *preview the text*. They do this by researching
- How long it is.
- How it is organized.
- What kind of features it has.
- What hyperlinks it has and if those take you entirely out of the text.
- Where ads have been inserted.
- The author and publisher/organization.

When starting digital nonfiction, readers take a moment to *make a reading plan*. They do this by deciding
- Where they'll start.
- If/when they'll go out of the text.
- How they'll take notes.
- How often they'll pause to process.

Digital readers *use embedded tools and features critically* as they read. They do this wisely by monitoring
- The source and tone of "look up" information such as vocabulary and historical references.
- Where hyperlinks take them and how to return to the original text.
- When features might be carefully tailored ads.

Digital readers know that their brain will be reluctant to reread, so they are extra *careful to attend to understanding*. They can do this by
- Noticing when their attention wanders.
- Using tools to reread often.
- Annotating in the text.
- Note taking outside the text.
- Pausing often to summarize.

Creating Tools and Edtech Spaces to Support Students Who Read Below Benchmark

You will have students who find reading hard, in both print and digital texts. Here is where AI can be a really helpful tool creator, especially if you teach older students and your classroom doesn't typically have a lot of accessible and yet still enticing books for preteens and teens. Reading can get all wrapped up in self-esteem, and it's hard for young people to admit that reading is challenging. Heck, it's hard for anyone to admit that they find something hard that others don't seem to, especially something they are asked to do every day, all day. Kids have to read in math; they have to read in science; they have to read in music. They have to read in the language that is the classroom language, even if that is not the language they are confident in. It can all get overwhelming for young people, and if you are an English teacher after 3rd grade, it's pretty overwhelming for you, too. Your curriculum is no longer one of reading instruction. It's a deep comprehension and interpretation curriculum, a close reading curriculum, and a writing about reading curriculum, inevitably.

We've spent a lot of time with teachers, exploring how AI might help us with readers who read way below benchmark. We encourage you to do the same, as colleagues will have new ideas, and AI will constantly have new capacities. Our goal isn't to circumvent intervention; these readers need assessment-based intervention that addresses why reading is so hard. Our goals here are to (1) create texts that readers who still need to practice emergent reading skills can read, and (2) support students in accessing texts the class is reading, such as whole-class texts, book club texts—any and all shared reading experiences.

Creating Texts for Readers: Decodables, Dual Language Stories, Illustrated Stories

Creating personal decodable texts for reluctant readers who need practice decoding is a great opportunity for AI to be your partner. Alexa, for instance, teaches at PS 158. She had a student who needed to practice cvc and ccvc words even as the main classroom curriculum had students in book clubs. This student (we'll call him Jack) *loved* Minecraft. Alexa asked ChatGPT to write a story using only cvc and ccvc words and simple high-frequency words (*look, the, they, are*) about Minecraft, with a focus on /ck/.

Alexa's AI partner produced:

> ### ✨ Jack and Rick in Minecraft
>
> Jack and Rick like to play Minecraft. They are best pals. One day, Jack and Rick look at the map. They see a big rock. "Let's go!" said Jack. Rick nods. The path is thick with trees. They hack and cut. Jack and Rick are quick. They find the big rock. It is black and has gold. "Look at that!" said Rick. Jack and Rick pick at the rock. They get a sack and pack the gold. "We are rich!" said Jack. They look at the sun. It is getting low. "We must go back," said Rick. They pack up and run back. The path is thick, but they are quick. Jack and Rick get back to the hut. They look at the gold and grin. "That was fun," said Jack. "Yes, it was," said Rick. They nap and dream of more gold. The end.

Let's consider, for a moment, all that Alexa has already accomplished. She and her AI partner have created a story that Jack is likely to want to read, because it's about characters he knows well (Jack himself and his friend), and the story arc is set inside a game that he adores. Meanwhile, Jack gets decoding practice, working inside a controlled text.

You could continue to innovate from here. You might, for instance, if Jack is an older reader, introduce several chapters so that this narrative becomes longer. You might add illustrations to make the text more engaging and accessible. For instance, when we asked ChatGPT image generator to illustrate the scene in the story where the boys see the rock just off the path, near the thick trees, and the scene where they pack the gold, our AI partner generated images that were gorgeous and enticing. Visit ai-enhancedliteracy.org to see the full ChatGPT image generation chat and prompts.

These images transform this story into something an older reader might still find exciting. We could continue to personalize these images, with skin tones, hair, and clothing styles that match the readers themselves, so that they see themselves in the stories they read.

Now let's explore how an AI partner might help us support readers with an English-only, print-only text, like Langston Hughes's *Thank You, M'am*, that the whole class will read. This situation, of facing a whole-class text, is one of the hardest for students who find print hard. Wrapped up in the task itself

Deepening Reading Comprehension with Digital Texts and Tools 103

are assumptions that all students can read the text and that they'll have equal access to the curriculum. We know enough about reading challenges to know that kind of equity simply won't be true. Even when the text is culturally relevant, even when it is chosen not only for its significance but, in the case of this story, for its brevity, it will pose significant challenges for some students. Here are some ways AI can help teachers and students tackle these challenges:

1. Ask your AI partner to create a story map that you can use as a starting point to introduce the story to some students, and they can use it to refer to. Ask your AI partner to translate this story map into various languages.
2. Ask your AI partner to translate the story (you may need to do this in parts). Ask your AI partner to also provide explanations of how it translated idioms.
3. Ask your AI partner to generate images for the text.
4. Create a dual language, illustrated version of the text.

Some of these tasks will be simple. For instance, when we asked AI to create a variety of translations in Ukrainian and a story map in Mandarin, that was easily done.

 These are the opening paragraphs of "Thank You, M'am" by Langston Hughes. Please translate them into Ukrainian:

She was a large woman with a large purse that had everything in it but hammer and nails. It had a long strap, and she carried it slung across her shoulder. It was about eleven o'clock at night, and she was walking alone, when a boy ran up behind her and tried to snatch her purse. The strap broke with the single tug the boy gave it from behind. But the boy's weight and the weight of the purse combined caused him to lose his balance so, instead of taking off full blast as he had hoped, the boy fell on his back on the sidewalk, and his legs flew up. The large woman simply turned around and kicked him right square in his blue-jeaned sitter. Then she reached down, picked the boy up by his shirt front, and shook him until his teeth rattled.

After that the woman said, "Pick up my pocketbook, boy, and give it here." She still held him. But she bent down enough to permit him to stoop and pick up her purse. Then she said, "Now ain't you ashamed of yourself?"

 Here is the translation of the opening paragraphs of **"Thank You, Ma'am"** into Ukrainian:

Дякую, мадам (Ленгстон Г'юз)

Вона була великою жінкою з великою сумкою, в якій було все, крім молотка і цвяхів. У неї був довгий ремінець, і вона носила її через плече. Було близько одинадцятої години вечора, і вона йшла одна, коли хлопець підбіг ззаду і спробував вирвати в неї сумку. Ремінець обірвався від одного ривка, який хлопець зробив ззаду. Але його власна вага разом із вагою сумки змусили його втратити рівновагу, тож, замість того, щоб утекти, як він сподівався, хлопець впав на спину на тротуар, а його ноги злетіли вгору.

Велика жінка просто обернулася і вдарила його прямо в його зад у джинсах. Потім вона нахилилася, схопила хлопця за передню частину сорочки і струснула його так, що у нього затріщали зуби.

Після цього жінка сказала:
— Підніми мою сумку, хлопче, і дай її сюди.

Вона все ще тримала його. Але нахилилася достатньо, щоб він міг нагнутися і підняти її сумку. Тоді вона сказала:
— Ну хіба тобі не соромно?

Here are a few idioms and figurative expressions from the original text and how they were translated into Ukrainian:

1. **"Had everything in it but hammer and nails"**
   - **Meaning**: This is a humorous exaggeration, suggesting that Mrs. Jones's purse was so full of various items that the only things missing were tools like a hammer and nails.
   - **Translation**: В якій було все, крім молотка і цвяхів.
   - **Explanation**: This keeps the humor while staying true to the original meaning.
2. **"Took off full blast"**
   - **Meaning**: To run away as fast as possible
   - **Translation**: Втекти, як він сподівався.
   - **Explanation**: Instead of translating literally (which might sound unnatural in Ukrainian), I conveyed the intended meaning—that the boy wanted to escape quickly.
3. **"Kicked him right square in his blue-jeaned sitter"**
   - **Meaning**: "Sitter" is a humorous way to refer to the boy's backside (his buttocks), and "blue-jeaned" specifies that he is wearing jeans. The phrase means that Mrs. Jones kicked him directly in the rear.
   - **Translation**: Вдарила його прямо в його зад у джинсах.
   - **Explanation**: I translated this in a way that keeps the meaning but removes the idiomatic complexity to make it clear to Ukrainian readers.
4. **"Shook him until his teeth rattled"**
   - **Meaning**: She shook him very forcefully, emphasizing her anger and his helplessness.
   - **Translation**: Струснула його так, що у нього затріщали зуби.
   - **Explanation**: I kept the vivid imagery while ensuring it made sense in Ukrainian.
5. **"Now ain't you ashamed of yourself?"**
   - **Meaning**: This rhetorical question is used to scold the boy, implying that he should feel guilty about his actions.
   - **Translation**: Ну хіба тобі не соромно?
   - **Explanation**: This is a direct translation that retains the same effect.

✦ Story Map in English and Mandarin

English	Mandarin
Boy attempts to steal Mrs. Jones' purse → Fails	男孩试图偷琼斯太太的钱包 → 失败
Mrs. Jones catches the boy	琼斯太太抓住了男孩
Mrs. Jones takes the boy to her home	琼斯太太带男孩回家
Mrs. Jones talks to the boy and learns his name is Roger	琼斯太太与男孩交谈,得知他叫罗杰
Mrs. Jones has Roger wash his face	琼斯太太让罗杰洗脸
Mrs. Jones cooks dinner for Roger	琼斯太太为罗杰做晚餐
They eat and talk	他们边吃边聊
Mrs. Jones gives Roger $10 for blue suede shoes	琼斯太太给罗杰10美元买蓝色麂皮鞋
Mrs. Jones sends Roger away with advice	琼斯太太送罗杰离开,并给予忠告
Roger leaves, grateful but unable to fully express his thanks	罗杰离开,心存感激但无法充分表达谢意

Asking our AI partner first to illustrate a few key scenes needs a bit more human mediation. For example, our AI partner generated three options. Visit ai-enhancedliteracy.org for the images.

The first one our AI partner generated seemed sensationalized and ultra violent because it showed a boy violently fighting with an older woman (which is not to say that kids wouldn't like it, but it feels like we might be taking liberties with Langston Hughes's vision). The second one seemed stereotypical and culturally damaging because it showed a woman looking like the original Aunt Jemima depiction. But the third has potential. It showed a well-dressed woman and a young boy, both in contemporary clothing. It feels respectful while also illuminating a scene. You will want to play a bit to get the kind of illustrations you were hoping for. Fortunately, you can give your AI partner feedback and choose the style that feels best. You can also improve it, if you'd like. For instance, each time your image generator makes an image, it will ask you if you want adjustments. You can say, "Yes, I'm concerned about this image feeling like it reiterates cultural stereotypes. Please make Mrs. Jones look like a well-dressed, contemporary, confident woman" or "Please avoid violent imagery that sensationalizes." We had to do this much revision because we were creating images before the newer versions of image generation. The newest version of ChatGPT (4.0) allows multimodal image generation, which puts AI in charge of creating images. That means you can expect images to be more intelligent and precise.

What matters here is that images, particularly, are powerful for increasing engagement. And they can also reiterate stereotypes or cultivate sensationalized interpretations of the text. Bring the same criticality and care to this work that you would to creating text sets or to choosing texts.

You can also ask your AI partner to create a trailer of a text or a summary. These summations can serve as text introductions, which are very helpful for students who will find the text itself challenging. The one adaptation we are cautious with is the multilevel text. Yes, your AI partner can make a text easier. It usually does this by simplifying the vocabulary and syntax and sometimes the structure. What's tricky about this kind of simplification is that often, the text itself is altered. If you are working with a nonfiction text, sometimes the ideas become oversimplified, losing the nuance that was important to the author's argument or stance. When you find yourself having to hugely simplify texts for students, ask yourself if that is the right text for that student. For instance, we love the way NewsELA can engage students with current events. Students who read at different levels can inform themselves and talk with each other about breaking news. And we're aware that in making the text simpler, we are not actually giving students the same access to ideas and vocabulary.

So it's one tool, just like the decodables we made are one tool. And we'd want students to have access to complex audio texts and visual texts and texts that are well-written at their level, so that they can both fully access the curriculum and gradually move up levels of complexity.

Creating Edtech Chat Rooms for Readers

Finally, remember you can create edtech AI chat discussions for your students around texts. These are incredibly supportive of students' comprehension. In a personal chat discussion, students often ask comprehension questions they wouldn't ask in class. They might ask how chapters of a novel are connected, or they sometimes ask about parts they find confusing. They often ask about vocabulary or concepts in a nonfiction text. They might ask to discuss the text first in their strongest language. All of these interactions with an AI partner can deepen students' understanding and engagement.

You might, for instance, design your edtech chat so it begins by saying to readers, "Let's talk about this story. What parts were you most struck by?" Or it could begin, "What did you think about the character of the boy in the story? Were you surprised by his actions?" Then your edtech AI can engage students in a deep discussion, supporting comprehension as needed and interpretation as readers show readiness. You'll also be able to see all those discussions and read your edtech partner's reports on them. Visit the website ai-enhanced literacy.org for examples of student discussions in edtech classrooms.

AI-generated reading supports like examples in Figure 4.3 are ones you can also teach students to create for themselves as well, inside an edtech chat, where they can get feedback. All learners can find themselves in situations where a text is challenging, and a summary, a preview, or a translation would be helpful. You might introduce these tools, for instance, when students are in book clubs, as a way to support all learners.

Accepting a Digital Future for Reading

Our final message about digital reading is that it is challenging, it can be beautiful, and it is the very near future. We are teachers. We adore print. We love the leather-bound novel, the first edition, the paper map that we carefully refold. And we know that stepping back from digital texts and digital reading is like stepping back from cell phones. It's unlikely to happen, and a generation of students awaits our full participation in helping them be as powerful as possible in these new modalities.

Figure 4.3
AI-Generated Tools to Support Readers

Tool	Example
Personalized decodable texts	AI can help write and illustrate decodable texts around students' interests and identities. These can support older readers who still need decoding practice and readers who are otherwise reluctant to read decodable texts. AI can create multiple chapters, making personalized, chapter book versions of decodable texts.
Story maps	AI can generate story maps, in multiple languages, for fiction and narrative nonfiction that students need to read for class. You can use these story maps to introduce texts and as reference points while students are reading. They can also serve as exemplars for creating story maps.
Illustrations	AI can generate illustrations for fiction and nonfiction texts, making these texts more engaging and accessible for students. You will need to preview and adjust these illustrations to ensure they are culturally responsive and appropriate. You can also adjust the style of illustrations to match the age and interest of the reader (e.g., making a decodable into a manga style).
Previews, trailers, and summaries	AI can generate a preview or trailer for a text, as a way to help students orient themselves to what they will read. A brief preview can increase engagement and accessibility, especially when combined with an illustration.
Translations	AI can provide translations of texts that students will read for class, supporting newcomers and multilingual learners. AI can also translate story maps and summaries. Readers might read a text first in the language they are most confident in. Or you can make a dual language version (including a dual language illustrated version) of a text using AI, so that newcomers can look between languages to access content. AI can also translate previews and summaries as helpful tools for multilingual learners, to orient them to a text.
Discussions with an edtech AI partner	Edtech AI allows students to discuss texts with an AI thought partner. Readers can get support with comprehension and vocabulary, they can test their ideas, and they can explore how parts of a text are connected. AI can speak with them in different languages as well, to support multilingual learners as they make sense of a text. Edtech AI chat discussions help students rehearse their thinking and deepen their understanding of texts. They can be very effective preparation for partnership, club, and class discussions.

Look at your curriculum for moments when you might insert some attention to digital reading practices. Perhaps you'd like to pilot a round of audiobook clubs. Perhaps you'd like to insert a podcast unit of study. Perhaps you'd like to use digital texts for some of your read-aloud instruction. It takes practice to develop deep reading practices with digital texts, and we need to begin that practice with students now. Look, too, for how you might insert some digital tools to support readers. Invite students to use image generators to illustrate favorite scenes. Ask your AI partner to create storyboards to support multilingual learners. Use edtech AI spaces for students to discuss texts and get support with comprehension. Meanwhile, you can continue to give beautiful books as presents, carry worn paperbacks around, and live as a lover of words!

Extending Multilingual Competencies

Generative AI can be a transformative democratic force in multilingual classrooms. It allows monolingual teachers to communicate with students and families, see students' competencies much more fully, and become more linguistically flexible. It allows students to bridge language differences immediately, in spoken and written form, so that they can participate in the curriculum, learn about one another's experiences and ideas, and develop linguistic flexibility. It allows students whose language skills in the classroom language limit their expression to translanguage and translate so that others hear their ideas and fully see these students. For transcending language differences and dismantling linguistic hierarchies and inequities, AI changes everything.

We'll look here at five ways classroom teachers can add AI-powered translation tools to the tools they and their students (and families) use to deepen the learning not only of multilingual students but of all students. One note about translation apps. We especially like DeepL and Google Translate for how easy they are to use, for how they translate spoken language as well as written language, and for their range of languages. We also like iTranslate and Microsoft Translator. We love the translation capability of edtech sites like Flint. But the most important thinking you'll do won't be about what app or platform to use; it will be about ways to incorporate translation tools to deepen learning and communication. We've found that the most powerful ways (see Figure 5.1) to use AI-powered translation tools include the following:

- Creating communities of care and belonging.
- Embracing AI-powered tools to more fully grasp and deepen students' critical competencies.
- Harnessing AI-powered translation tools and sites to foster peer discussion and learning alliances.
- Increasing teachers' knowledge of linguistics.
- Teaching with linguistic flexibility and cultural competence.

Creating Communities of Care and Belonging

There are beautiful voices in multilingual education that teach us so much about creating communities of care and belonging. Let's look at a few of these voices to lay the groundwork for creating these kinds of empathetic communities. Carla España and Luz Yadira Herrera, in *En Comunidad: Lessons for Centering the Voices and Experiences of Bilingual Latinx Students* (2020), advocate for bilingual pedagogy that honors students' language practices and linguistic and cultural heritages. They ask teachers to think about ways to create liberating spaces. They make suggestions for using storytelling as a way for students to share their perspectives and histories, they show how to curate text sets that center students' identities, and they look carefully at how sustaining pedagogies can wrap students in acceptance and love.

María Paula Ghiso and Gerald Campano, in *Methods for Community-Based Research: Advancing Educational Justice and Epistemic Rights* (2024), frame education as a community endeavor, showing teachers how to partner with families and community members so that literacy deepens cultural awareness, forwards social justice, and becomes a reciprocal process. They describe the power of a "local intellectual commons," a site where community members share knowledge and engage in study and inquiry. The metaphor of an intellectual commons is beautiful for multilingual classrooms, in how it conceptualizes the classroom as a site of reciprocal learning.

Ofelia García and colleagues in *The Translanguaging Classroom: Leveraging Student Bilingualism for Learning* (2017), and in García and Kleifgen (2020), share a vision for educational spaces that bolster students' language acquisition in all their languages. They advocate for a more democratic sense of language, one in which primacy isn't placed implicitly and explicitly, again and again, on a new classroom language versus the many languages that students and families bring to school.

We love these educators' call to make our classrooms more humane and equitable, and we think that AI can help. We see how the first barrier that gets in the way of students and families being more fully seen and known is often

Figure 5.1
Harnessing AI to Deepen Linguistic Competencies

How Can AI Help You Create Communities of Care and Belonging?	How Can AI Help You More Fully Grasp and Deepen Students Competencies?	How Can AI-Powered Translation Tools Help You Foster Peer Discussion and Learning Alliances?	How Can AI Help You Increase Your Knowledge of Linguistics?
Invite students and families to share their stories, and use AI to translate these stories into many languages.	Invite students to write for you in the language they are most confident in, and translate it with an AI-translation tool.	Figure out which of your students are adept with technology, and set them up to be UN-style translator partners with newcomers.	Ask your AI partner to teach you about cognates in your students' languages.
Choose a community read text, and use AI to translate this text into the languages of your families.	Use AI to help you create multilingual text sets.	Give tech-philic young people a role in class as experts.	Ask your AI partner for suggestions of common compound words across languages.
Seek narratives from your students' cultural heritages, and use AI to translate them.	Use AI to translate all-class texts, and students' responses to these, so that you fully grasp students' thinking.	Set up discussion groups that begin with edtech AI chat discussion partners.	Ask your AI partner to provide culturally relevant examples of idioms.
Ask students and their families to share their hopes and dreams, using AI as a translator.	Set up school-based AI chat rooms for students to engage in discussion.	Teach writing partners to use AI to translate their writing so their peer writing partner can access it.	Ask your AI partner to collect domain vocabulary in more than one language.
Make it a habit to translate communications to parents and caregivers.			Ask your AI partner to research etymology and morphology.

a language barrier. We think of how often we, as teachers, do not speak the languages of some of our students, and therefore are less able to wrap these students in care and understanding as we are with students who share our language. We think about how easily and quickly we not only reach out to but create bonds of understanding with those parents and caregivers with whom we communicate without linguistic effort. And we know this isn't fair and it isn't right. Our aim, then, is to explore ways to harness the swiftness and vastness of AI to democratize access, agency, and critical participation for multilingual students and therefore deepen the educational experiences of all in the community.

Invite Students and Families to Share Their Stories, and Use AI to Translate These Stories into Many Languages

You might design a community storytelling moment, invite students to interview family members, teach memoir workshops in school and in the community, invite teachers to interview families, or make personal narrative the first writing unit in each grade as school opens. A teacher, for instance, might share a personal narrative and use AI to translate it into the many languages of her classroom community, so that her students and families know her through her story. Students might tell their stories orally, and AI can translate them, either orally or transforming them into written forms. In "Liberatory Education: Integrating the Science of Learning and Culturally Responsive Practice," Zaretta Hammond (2021) describes centering a writing classroom on students' language experiences so that they become leaders of their own learning. We need many ways to learn from our students so that they can learn from and with us.

Ghiso and colleagues (2024) describe how "students from immigrant backgrounds often enter culturally and linguistically assimilationist educational contexts" (p. 497). These environments may be overtly xenophobic and assimilationist, or more often, they can be repressive in less visible ways: in the discouragement of home language use, in unintended propagation of cultural stereotypes, and in all the mundane ways that young people can be positioned as "other" in school. Storytelling builds empathy. Maryanne Wolf (2018) has shown that one part of the brain that literally grows stronger through reading stories is the part that is responsible for empathy. Stories give us insight into others' experiences and histories and heritages. It is no small thing to collect families' stories and to use AI to make these readable to all.

Choose a Community Read Text, and Use AI to Translate This Text into the Languages of Your Families

The community read can be a poem, picture book, or short story. Send home the story and the translations so that children can read the story with their families, or record students reading the text aloud in the languages of their families. Invite families in for a shared storytelling moment, gathering around this text. Many gorgeous, significant picture books have been translated into many languages. These picture books open up discussions of friendship, moving to new places, speaking multiple languages, and finding beauty in neighborhoods and community. Visit ai-enhancedliteracy.org for a list of picture books that have been translated into many languages. Some languages remain at the edge of children's publishing, and you can use AI-powered translation tools to share these classroom stories with all children and families in your community.

Some picture books that could be beautiful community reads include the following:

- *Watercress,* written by Andrew Wang and illustrated by Jason Chin
- *My First Day*, written by Phùng Nguyên Quang and illustrated by Huynh Kim Liên
- *My Papi Has a Motorcycle*, written by Isabel Quintero and illustrated by Zeke Peña
- *Last Stop on Market Street,* written by Matt de la Peña and illustrated by Christian Robinson
- *Evelyn del Rey Is Moving Away,* written by Meg Medina and illustrated by Sonia Sanchez
- *The Day You Begin,* written by Jacqueline Woodson and illustrated by Rafael López
- *The Paper Bag Princess,* written by Robert Munsch and illustrated by Michael Martchenko

Seek Narratives from Your Students' Cultural Histories, and Use AI to Translate Them

Gather myths, legends, folktales, oral histories, and fairy tales. Invite students to read and tell them in class to celebrate the diversity of histories and cultures in your community. Encourage them to think about connections across characters, places, and stories. You can also ask your AI partner to investigate the cross-cultural histories of fairytales and to recommend multiple versions.

Ask Students and Their Families to Share Their Hopes and Dreams, Using AI as a Translator

In *Not This but That: No More Teaching Without Positive Relationships*, Howard and colleagues (2020) describe the importance of what they call *aspirational capital*, asking how can people help children fulfill their hopes and dreams if they don't know what those are. AI translation tools can help you learn what the children who just arrived from Ukraine or Syria were dreaming for how they'll grow in your classroom and what they want to accomplish in the future, so that you can help them hold onto those dreams and find new ones as well.

Make It a Habit to Translate Communications to Parents and Caregivers

You saw in Chapter 3 how your AI partner can read student writing and generate a love note to parents about the beautiful work their child is doing. Ask AI to translate that note into Mandarin, Ukrainian, or whatever the language of the family is. We often write something like, "I'm eager to communicate with you about your child, who is doing some beautiful work in school. I used an AI partner to help me assess your student's writing and compose this note. Please forgive any awkwardness in translation. Here are some of the things your child is doing well...." That way, you've been transparent about how you use AI as an instructional support, and you'll be forgiven for how AI will translate your words exactly, as it tends to avoid idioms, making your language very formal.

Embracing AI-Powered Tools to More Fully Grasp and Deepen Students' Critical Competencies

If you've ever been a language learner, striving to express yourself in a language that still feels awkward on your tongue, you'll know how frustrating it can be to experience language as a constraint. It's hard to sparkle or be your full self while struggling to find words. Long after you are comfortable on the playground or athletic field, academic conversations are daunting. Many years ago, Danling Fu, who came from China to the United States and became a professor in multilingual education, wrote *My Trouble Is My English: Asian Students and the American Dream* (1995). One student whom Danling interviewed described how her words turned to snow in her mouth when she spoke English. We know that feeling, having lived and studied in places where the language of the classroom was not yet ours. It can feel like you are wearing your skin inside out, like you are both entirely bare and covered, never fully seen for your entire self.

AI can be a radical force in creating humane and respectful learning experiences for multilingual learners. You already know you can turn to AI to develop resources for students who are in earlier stages of language acquisition than others in the class, so that students have consistent opportunities to read and write English, or whatever the new classroom language is, at their level. In Chapter 3, we looked at how to partner with AI to create personalized decodable texts, as well as how AI can create multilevel texts for students. But those resources, and the idea that we are solely teaching a language, aren't enough. Multilingual learners, especially preteens and teens, also need to be able to participate in the classroom curriculum. They need to experience texts that are designed for their age level. They need to be able to express themselves fully, regardless of their stage of language acquisition in the classroom language. AI can make all of that more possible.

AI-powered translation tools can help recent immigrants and newcomers be seen and heard and have access to grade-level curriculum, by allowing fluidity in reading and writing in home languages while being understood through translation in the classroom language. As they begin to read and write in the classroom language, students may naturally translanguage as they use all their linguistic resources (Vogel & García, 2017). We ascribe to Vogel and García's positioning of translanguaging as a fluid and powerful linguistic response. It's important to have a conversation with students as they decide, as they begin to use translation tools and write in the classroom language, which words they would not translate. Many of our students, for instance, neither translate nor explain words like *abuela* and *café con leche* in the stories they write in or translate to English, just as so many published writers also assert the duality of their linguistic repertoires and identities. When we look at translating student writing (and allowing students to write in their most powerful languages) here, then, it is so that teachers (especially teachers who consider themselves monolingual) may understand more of students' thinking, grasp more of their literacy competencies, and create opportunities for students to engage in critical thinking beyond their current expressiveness in the classroom language.

Here are a few ways to make AI a transformative partner in creating challenging learning experiences for multilingual learners that respect their critical capacities.

Invite Students to Write for You in the Language They Are Most Confident in, and Translate It with an AI-Translation Tool

For instance, we have invited students to write a literary essay about a wordless digital narrative or picture book (removing all language barriers) in their strongest language. Then we use DeepL, iTranslate, or Google Translate (or edtech such as Flint) to read that piece in English. You find out so much. You learn what that student is thinking about the text. You learn about their control of essay structure. You learn about their literary and academic vocabulary. Now you're able to say to that student, "I see what you can do when you are writing in Spanish/Ukrainian/Mandarin/Arabic, and I want to compliment you on... and it feels like as a writer, what's next for you might be...."

In *Rooted in Strength: Using Translanguaging to Grow Multilingual Readers and Writers,* Espinosa and Ascenzi-Moreno remind us that "emergent bilingual children need to know that their voices matter and that their voices can be developed—that their writing can help them make sense of the world as they use it to learn and wonder about them" (2021, p. 141). For a preteen or teen writer who finds writing in the classroom language limiting, it's important for them to be able to be known as a writer and to learn more about themselves and the world by writing, with their full powers.

You will have such a stronger grasp of students' writing competencies and what they are thinking when they show you in their strongest language. Celebrate and deepen these competencies. Know that growth in one language will be reflected by growth in another, so if you coach a student to raise the level of their essay in Ukrainian, that will ultimately serve them well. Meanwhile, you can also say, "Let's look at what's next for you as a writer in English, or your new language...." That writing might be at a very different level, and you may find yourself teaching primary writing lessons. But it is going to be so much less daunting for a young person to sketch and label and write on primary paper in a new language, if they are also being fully seen as a writer across languages.

Use AI to Help You Create Multilingual Text Sets

Students can learn content at their learning level while they are acquiring a new language at a more novice level. Know that even if they will be discussing sea turtles or photosynthesis or Malala in English, learning a lot about the topic in any language will help them build content understanding. Once they have these understandings, they can begin to read texts in English or the classroom language as well—and they'll be able to do so with more ease and fluency because they have content knowledge. Edtech AI such as Flint lets you set up students to read and discuss in multiple languages, before translating their thinking into English or making discussion notes in English for students.

We usually create Padlets for content studies and recently found ourselves creating many in Spanish and French for various teachers. Here are some tips we can pass along. Use DeepL, Google Translate, or an app of your choice to help you find search terms in your target language. For instance, a class of 6th graders studying the Middle Ages included newcomers whose most powerful language was Spanish. We put into DeepL terms like "Middle Ages," "feudalism," "daily life in the Middle Ages," and so on. Then we put these now-translated-into-Spanish terms into YouTube as "La Edad Media para niños" and so on to find educational videos. It's always helpful to start with "for children" so that you find accessible texts. In moments, we had an accessible text set. In Chapter 6, you'll learn how AI can also help you build these text sets.

Visit the website ai-enhancedliteracy.org for sample Padlets to support content studies.

Use AI to Translate All-Class Texts, and Students' Responses to These, So That You Fully Grasp Students' Thinking

For instance, if the whole class is reading Langston Hughes's *Thank You, M'am*, ask your AI partner to translate this text into multilingual learners' languages. Invite them to read, talk, and write about it first in those languages in an edtech site, such as Flint, that allows many languages. Your edtech AI partner can help you read those responses so that you know how your students think about things like characterization, theme, and authors' craft, as well as the social issues embedded in the texts your class is studying. AI translation tools will let you know these students' full ideas—something that was cumbersome to impossible until recently. These same students can then study the text in English as well, but they'll do so already knowing the text and confident that their thinking is expressed and valued. This kind of access to grade-level curriculum is essential for students to develop their critical capacities. While they are learning the language, especially for young adults, they also need to develop their critical-thinking skills and work with sophisticated texts. AI makes that possible.

Set Up School-Based AI Chat Rooms for Students to Engage in Discussion

Use MagicSchool, SchoolAI, Flint, or any of the many school versions of generative AI to provide students with an AI thought partner. When you set up these chats, allow for secondary languages. For instance, in one of our high schools, we set up Flint as an AI partner for 9th graders, so that each student could discuss their ideas about *The Catcher in the Rye* before their book club discussions. This 9th grade is in an international school, and while all the kids were reading the novel in English, some immediately asked if they could develop their ideas first in other languages before they go to their book club discussion in English. Flint allows for Russian, Spanish, and Dutch, which were the three languages these students asked for. They each developed their thinking in those languages, with Flint as a partner. Flint would say things like, "Have you also thought about…" and "Perhaps you should think about Chapter x…" as we had set it up to push students to develop their ideas and their evidence—in Russian or Dutch, which we could not do. Near the close of these AI-partnered discussions, students asked their AI partner to help them translate their thinking into English, and they used these notes to rehearse for their book club.

The most important pedagogical decision here is to harness AI for students to deepen their thinking using all their languages and to use it to help them translate that thinking into the classroom language—creating more access, inclusivity, and equity in the curriculum.

Harnessing AI-Powered Translation Tools and Sites to Foster Peer Discussion and Learning Alliances

So far, we've explored how to use AI-powered translation tools so that teachers can access students' skills and thinking across language barriers. You can use those same tools to make it possible for students to engage with their peers across language divides. Kids already do this in the playground and on the playing field. It takes young people minutes to learn the local word for *goal*, *out*, and *score* when they get on a soccer field. It's amazing, really, to see kids share and learn highly technical, specific vocabulary, when they are doing something they love.

You want to achieve that same fluency with communication inside the classroom, even as academic language remains a challenge. It's just as important that students can fully express their thinking to each other as it is so that they can communicate with their teachers. Translation apps can support increased communication with and among multilingual learners (Lake & Beisly, 2019). Here are some ways AI can help deepen student communication.

Figure Out Which of Your Students Are Adept with Technology, and Set Them Up to Be UN-Style Translator Partners with Newcomers

For instance, if Partner A speaks Mandarin and is the sole Mandarin speaker in class, Partner B is there to help, along with their AI partner, which might be GoogleTranslate or a school AI such as MagicSchool or Flint. Using speech translation and written translation, Partner B can use their tech abilities to ensure that Partner A understands what the class is doing, help them get started, translate classroom work into Mandarin, and translate Partner A's work from Mandarin into the classroom language.

Give Tech-Philic Young People a Role in Class as Experts

There are almost always young people who are more adept than adults in the class with technology, including the rapid use of AI-powered translation apps. Celebrate their tech expertise and give them roles in the community. They can offer seminars for students on using translation apps. They can explore the variety of tools available and make recommendations. They can explore the capacities of school-sponsored AI, including what languages are translated and how easily these school platforms support rapid translation.

Set Up Discussion Groups That Begin with Edtech AI Chat Discussion Partners

These discussions with an AI partner allow multilingual learners to rehearse their thinking in all their languages. Because these discussions are written, they are easily translated, which means a peer discussion group might read one student's translated thinking, translate their own thinking into that student's language, and talk to one another about their classwork across language divides. Students view one another differently when they have access to the full range of one another's intellects. AI can help make that happen.

Teach Writing Partners to Use AI to Translate Their Writing So Their Peer Writing Partner Can Access It

Those student partners now have a much better idea of what their writing partner can do as a writer: There will be more respect, more understanding of what they each have to say, more inclusion, more equity. Then when writers are also writing in the new language of the classroom, which is often writing at a more novice level, they know their partner has already seen their capacities and heard their voice.

Increasing Teachers' Knowledge of Linguistics

There are many linguistic connections that you could be making, as teachers, to support your multilingual learners that you miss because you are monolingual or not especially knowledgeable about the languages your students speak. Learning from an AI partner can help highlight these connections and highlight when language patterns are different. AI can help you be better prepared to teach vocabulary, grammar, etymology, and morphology not only to multilingual learners but to all your learners.

Here are a few ways AI can support linguistic development, by deepening teachers' linguistic knowledge: cognates, compound words, idioms, domain vocabulary, etymology, and morphology.

Ask Your AI Partner to Teach You About Cognates in Your Students' Languages

Cognates are words that sound similar and share meaning across languages for the languages your children speak. If, for instance, you have students whose home language is Spanish, French, Italian, or Portuguese, there will be hundreds of cognates. For example, if a student knows the meaning of *importante* in Spanish or Italian, it's a small leap to understand *important* in English or French. You might begin by explaining what cognates are and giving some examples of how being alert to cognates can extend vocabulary knowledge across languages. Then give students an opportunity to do some rapid sorts of cognates, inviting them to notice spelling patterns as well. Studying cognates deepens vocabulary and linguistic flexibility.

Your AI partner can help you generate lists of cognates, which you can cut up so that students can sort them. Suggest that AI emphasize common words and those that suggest patterns across languages. Kids will notice patterns, for example, that it seems like words that end in *tion* in English seem to end in *ción* in Spanish. You can also ask your AI partner to teach you about cognate patterns and to give you lists of words that highlight those patterns.

Although you'll see the most cognates and the strongest patterns across Romance languages, your AI partner can teach you about words that are cognates in other languages as well. For instance, when we asked our AI partner to support us with learning about cognates in Russian and English, it taught us a bit about the origins of these languages as well as shared words. We're now better prepared to talk to our Russian-speaking students about being alert to cognates, and we know that there will be two kinds: Russian and English words that share the same derivation, and words that drift into Russian and English from other languages. You can visit one of our partner sites for printable collections of cognates that students can sort at vocabularyconnections.org.

 Yes, there *are* cognates across English and Russian! While English is a Germanic language with heavy Latin influence, and Russian is a Slavic language, they still share some vocabulary due to:

1. Shared Indo-European roots
2. International scientific/technical terms
3. Loanwords from one another (especially from English into Russian in modern times)

Here are a few types and examples of cognates:

• **True Cognates (Shared Indo-European Roots)**
These words have a common ancestor and evolved in both languages:

— мать (mat'): mother
— брат (brat): brother

- день (den'): day
- нога (noga): knee/leg (compare to "knee" in Old English: *cnēow*)

These words may not look or sound exactly the same anymore but come from the same ancient roots.

• **Loanword Cognates (Often from English to Russian)**
These words have been borrowed into Russian, usually in the 20th and 21st centuries:

- компьютер (komp'yuter): computer
- интернет (internet): internet
- телефон (telefon): telephone
- спорт (sport): sport
- футбол (futbol): football (soccer)

• **Scientific/International Terms**
Because of shared academic, medical, or technical roots (often from Latin or Greek):

- атом (atom): atom
- музыка (muzyka): music
- физика (fizika): physics
- биология (biologiya): biology

Ask Your AI Partner for Suggestions of Common Compound Words Across Languages

Understanding compound words helps students figure out the meanings of unfamiliar words by breaking them down into smaller, recognizable parts. Knowledge of compound words also aids spelling proficiency. AI can teach you common parts of compound words in English to help your multilingual learners build their word knowledge. It can also provide you with examples of compound words in other languages so that you can teach the idea of compound words across languages.

When you teach compound words, AI can also help you generate illustrated cards. For instance, we asked our AI partner to generate images to illustrate sea, star, and sea star. It gave us images (visit ai-enhancedliteracy.org) that we could print as cards or turn into a digital tool for students to create compound words with. It takes about five minutes for your AI partner to generate compound word lists and illustrate them. So much teacher time is saved. You can also visit one of our partner websites, vocabularyconnections.org, for printable collections of compound word cards.

Ask Your AI Partner to Provide Culturally Relevant Examples of Idioms

Often, when idioms are translated literally, the meaning is lost or becomes utterly confusing. For instance, when trying to translate the expression "it's raining cats and dogs," a literal translation leads nowhere. But you can ask AI to help you with culturally relevant parallel expressions. Here are some AI-assisted culturally relevant examples that our AI partner taught us:

- For a student from Mexico: "In Mexico, a similar expression is 'está lloviendo a cántaros,' which literally means 'it's raining pitchers.' Both expressions mean it's raining very heavily."
- For a student from China: "In Chinese, there's a saying '狂风暴雨' (kuángfēng bàoyǔ), which means 'fierce wind and violent rain.' This is used to describe very heavy rain, similar to 'raining cats and dogs'."
- For a student from Russia: "дождь стеной" (dozhd' stenoy), which means 'the rain is like a wall,' describing rain so heavy it appears to form a solid wall of water."

Understanding idioms helps language learners grasp cultural references. Idioms also offer insight into historical context and are conversation starters. When you use an idiom, in context, it creates a sense of naturalness and embeddedness. They are also fascinating. Your AI partner can give you a little college-level micro-lecture on idioms, and you'll find yourself asking more and more as you learn about the cultural origin of sayings.

Ask Your AI Partner to Collect Domain Vocabulary in More Than One Language

Just as it's helpful for multilingual students to have access to text sets in their most powerful language, it's also helpful for them to collect *domain vocabulary*—expert vocabulary related to content—in that language as they build knowledge. Sometimes, unless you're careful to create opportunities for students to acquire academic language in all their languages, they graduate with academic English and social Spanish, Arabic, or whatever their home language is. AI can help you and your students become more adept at gathering domain vocabulary in more than one language. For students, as they read texts in their most powerful language, they can begin to collect words that are important to this topic, and they can use AI to translate those words into English or the classroom language. That process will help students begin to be able to talk and write about this topic in English, using more expert vocabulary. It will also build their academic language and understanding in more than one language.

You, too, as a teacher, can turn to your AI partner to foster this process. For instance, knowing that Nico's first language is Russian, as you're reading aloud a text on climate and weather, you might have already printed some of the vocabulary in Russian, so that as the whole class learns new technical terms such as *heat index* and *sea level rise*, Nico learns them in Russian as well as English. AI makes this kind of preparation so easy. You might invite some students to be language curators, and as you dive into content studies, they can begin to collect and share domain vocabulary in many languages, using their classroom texts and AI as resources.

Ask Your AI Partner to Research Etymology and Morphology

Your AI partner can explain historical derivations of words, and it can suggest prefixes, suffixes, and roots to teach. It can help you plan to teach, for example, the 15 most common Greek and Latin prefixes and suffixes. It can be a research partner to you and your students when you want to explore the derivation of words students are curious about. For instance, when we ask our AI partner to suggest the order to teach prefixes to 5th graders, it orders them by frequency. It also gives some suggestions to think about for teaching prefixes—which match those of many linguists (Ehrenworth, 2025).

5 Essential Prefixes for Teaching Morphology
1. un- (not, opposite of)
   - unhappy, unclear, unfair, unlock
   - Teaches basic negation concept
2. re- (again, back)
   - rebuild, rewrite, return, repeat
   - Shows action being done again
3. dis- (not, opposite of, apart)
   - disagree, disappear, disconnect
   - Alternative way to show opposition
4. pre- (before)
   - preview, prevent, prepare, predict
   - Important for time-related concepts
5. in- (not, in/into)
   - incorrect, invisible, insert
   - Note: Also appears as il-, im-, ir- depending on root word

 Teaching Tips:
- Introduce prefixes gradually, starting with the most common (un-, re-, dis-)
- Use familiar words as examples first
- Create word walls showing prefix families
- Practice identifying prefixes in reading materials
- Have students create their own examples
- Show how the same prefix can be used with different root words

It's always interesting, though, to ask your AI partner why or how they came to their response. In this case, when we interrogated our AI partner, asking it to explain why these particular prefixes were deemed significant, it gave us this information:

Let me explain the selection criteria for these prefixes.

1. **Frequency of Use:** 'un-', 're-', and 'dis-' are among the most frequently occurring prefixes in English text. Students of school texts and general reading materials show these appear consistently across grade levels. For example, words like "unlock," "rewrite," and "disagree" appear regularly in 5th grade reading materials.
2. **Grade-Level Appropriateness:** These prefixes are typically included in grades 3–6 curriculum standards. They're complex enough to challenge 5th graders but not so advanced that they'll overwhelm them. By 5th grade, students are ready to move beyond the most basic prefixes to include ones like "inter-" and "trans-."
3. **Utility in Content Areas:** Several of these prefixes are crucial for understanding academic vocabulary:
   - "non-" and "anti-" are important for science (nonfiction, antibiotic)
   - "pre-" and "post-" help with historical timelines
   - "sub-" and "inter-" appear frequently in math and geography terms
4. **Clear, Consistent Meanings:** Most of these prefixes have relatively stable meanings, making them easier to learn and apply. For instance, "un-" consistently means "not" or "opposite of," unlike some more advanced prefixes that can have multiple meanings.
5. **Building Blocks:** These prefixes form the foundation for understanding more complex vocabulary later. For example, understanding "bi-" (two) helps students later learn "tri-" (three) and other numerical prefixes.
6. **Common in Student Writings:** These prefixes appear frequently in the types of words students this age are beginning to use in their own writing, like "misunderstand," "overexcited," or "interact."

It's a helpful explanation. Of course, we can compare to the discussions of morphology in other texts, such as *Vocabulary Connections: A Structured Approach to Deepening Students' Academic and Expressive Language* (Ehrenworth, 2025) and *Shifting the Balance, Grades 3–5: Six Ways to Bring the Science of Reading into the Upper Elementary Classroom* (Cunningham, 2023). But in the span of 10 seconds, our AI partner gives us a framework to think about.

Teaching with Linguistic Flexibility and Cultural Competence

Ultimately, there is no one, single way that AI makes classrooms more welcoming, more respectful, and more inclusive for multilingual learners and their families. It's that AI makes it easier to do things we've always been striving for: to reach out equally to all our families and caregivers, to build bridges to our communities, to fully grasp our students' competencies, to foster their academic growth in all their languages, to create opportunities for students to fully express themselves, and for learning to be reciprocal.

Vogel and García (2017) call for instruction that integrates students' in-school and out-of-school language practices and that values students' diverse language practices. Ghiso and colleagues (2024) call for a shared intellectual commons, an intellectual nexus in which classroom and community learning are not separated but are forged with bonds of curiosity, acceptance, and determination to achieve social justice, inside school and out. AI cannot do all of that for us. But we can use it for good. The ability to instantly translate language, research language, and communicate across language differences may seem like a small thing. But the very swiftness of this process with AI can shift our pedagogies so that our classrooms become ones where linguistic flexibility and cultural competence are embedded into the structures of the classroom.

Building and Using Text Sets

One way we make sense of the world is through collecting and curating. It starts from a young age. Children collect all sorts of things: toys, playing cards, books. Then they curate. They can tell you which toys are the best. They trade cards to strengthen and expand their collection, and they organize books by interest, author, theme, color, and size. When we see their collections, we gain valuable insights into the intricacies of LEGO, Pokémon, and manga—and how our kids understand and interact with the worlds they create. As educators, we recognize that the kids are doing more than pursuing their interests; they are building content literacy. They are learning vocabulary, building background knowledge, synthesizing information, and making meaning.

Reading comprehension and critical literacies are developed through a similar process. Texts feel more significant and weightier when read alongside other carefully selected texts. A poem when nestled among other poems, for instance, increases in meaning. Conversations about significant themes often surface when multiple life experiences are placed side-by-side. We quickly notice patterns, question assumptions, and engage with the complex dialogue unfolding across texts. And perhaps we even begin to feel more connected to the rest of the world, bound together much like the pages in a book.

Text sets create conditions for us, as readers, to be more engaged, make meaningful connections, and draw out deeper insights. They also accomplish a few important tasks in terms of increasing equity. First, a text set immediately introduces choice. In *Opening Minds,* Peter Johnston (2012) describes how choice is significant in increasing student engagement. When you introduce choice, you increase engagement, and that increases reading volume. Like an athlete who improves with sustained activity and practice, voluminous reading is similarly correlated with reading achievement (Allington & McGill-Franzen, 2021; Bergen et al., 2020; Coventry et al., 2023).

However, text sets do more than introduce choice and increase engagement. They allow you to increase criticality. A carefully curated text set introduces multiple perspectives, increases representation, deepens the diversity of voices, and amplifies the stances your students will engage with critically. A multiplicity of texts can interrupt single-perspective viewpoints by engaging readers to consider multiple stories and voices surrounding an event or experience.

Moreover, text sets significantly improve accessibility in your curriculum. By including multimodal texts in the form of audio, video, and interactive sites, as well as translated texts, you give curricular access to newcomers, multilingual learners, and students who find print hard. Text sets are magical.

AI is now a powerful ally in this process. AI technology helps you curate diverse, engaging, and accessible text sets by helping you find (and generate) texts with greater ease across a wide array of modalities. In this chapter, we'll focus on the following:

- Creating text sets that add multiple perspectives and resources to a whole-class novel.
- Anticipating (and minimizing) hallucinations and cultural flattening.
- Curating text sets on nonfiction topics.
- Orienting students to new topics and text.
- Inviting students to co-create book club text sets.
- Embracing text sets to foster choice, student agency, and analysis.

Creating Text Sets That Add Multiple Perspectives and Resources to a Whole-Class Novel

One scenario where text sets can have a large impact is during whole-class novel instruction. Shared experiences with a common text foster grand discussions, build community, and provide a common experience in a text that can become a reference point when studying stories in the future. However, relying solely on a single text also limits diverse perspectives, fails to engage all readers when interests and abilities vary, and may not adequately address the diverse learning needs and backgrounds of all students in the classroom.

Let's imagine how AI can help create a more inclusive, multi-perspective text set to surround a whole-class novel. In our class, students are reading *The Giver* by Lois Lowry, a widely read dystopian novel that follows Jonas as he explores individuality and conformity as he learns the true cost of living in a seemingly perfect society governed by Sameness. It's fascinating, and for some readers, it's hard. We also know that many authors have also written on the themes of personal identity, societal compliance, and societal pressure from a variety of differing perspectives and experiences.

Let's prompt AI. For this example, we'll use Claude. We could also use ChatGPT, Gemini, or any other available large language model. Notice how we use specific language to prompt AI to create a text set with a wide range of voices and perspectives. We also want AI to justify its choices by providing a rationale and a connection to our central text, *The Giver*.

 I'm teaching *The Giver* by Lois Lowry to 8th graders. Please suggest a diverse range of short texts (excerpts, articles, poems, etc.) that provide multiple perspectives on the themes of conformity, individuality, and social control. Include BIPOC authors, neurodivergent voices, and contemporary youth perspectives. For each suggestion, provide a brief rationale for its inclusion and how it connects to *The Giver*. Fact-check sources for accuracy and grade-level appropriateness.

It almost always pays off to be more specific in your prompting. Treat your AI partner like a very willing, very skilled student teacher. In this prompt, we are making sure we provide lots of specific context. We use precise language by specifying our core novel, the grade level of our class, and specific categories we want AI to draw upon.

As directed, Claude gives us recommendations, a rationale, and the connection to our central text, *The Giver*. For simplicity, we've reorganized Claude's response into Figure 6.1.

Figure 6.1
AI-Generated Diverse Text Set for Teaching *The Giver*

Title	Rationale	Connection
"The Mask" by Maya Angelou (poem)	This poem explores the idea of hiding one's true self to conform to societal expectations, mirroring Jonas's journey of discovering his true identity.	Relates to the theme of conformity in *The Giver* and how characters suppress their individuality
Excerpt from *The Hate U Give* by Angie Thomas (novel)	This contemporary YA novel deals with themes of identity and speaking out against injustice in a controlled society.	Parallels Jonas's struggle to confront the flaws in his seemingly perfect community
"Harrison Bergeron" by Kurt Vonnegut (short story)	This satirical story presents a society where everyone is forced to be equal, taking conformity to an extreme.	Offers a different perspective on the pursuit of sameness seen in *The Giver*
Same but Different by Holly Robinson Peete, Ryan Elizabeth Peete, and RJ Peete (book)	This book, written by neurodivergent co-authors, provides an authentic perspective on growing up with autism.	Encourages students to reflect on what it means to be different in a controlled society
Float (animated short film)	This short film metaphorically portrays the challenges of raising a neurodivergent child and the pressures to conform.	Fosters discussion about individuality and acceptance—similar to Jonas's struggle to embrace his differences

We appreciate that our AI partner includes some texts we know but didn't think to connect to *The Giver*. Being reminded of texts we already love and have on hand is helpful. It's easy to get locked into well-worn paths and miss opportunities to update the curriculum by taking advantage of new text pairings. It also gives us a sense of affirmation.

Also, AI is introducing us to some texts that we are less familiar with and can't wait to explore. We encourage you to take on a similar approach, by reading responses with similar lenses and asking, What is affirming? What's a new possibility? The vast knowledge of AI makes it a particularly helpful ally when looking for new text recommendations. There is a chance that we'll see combinations of texts that transcend suggested reading lists as the algorithms generate responses to our requests.

We also suggest you regularly visit your local librarian or school's media specialist, who can be helpful in suggesting and finding books that are perfect for the local context of your classroom, but who can also give hands-on assistance with the logistics of getting copies into kids' hands. These colleagues can also help you carefully consider how these texts would serve your particular students. They'll also be using AI, and they'll curate these AI recommendations through their personal experiences. Finally, you'll need to assess the texts you put in front of students for accessibility, appropriateness, and potential for genuine engagement. This critical analysis is an essential part of your role—and you can get enormous help from an AI partner with getting started.

Consider the various ways you might incorporate suggested texts into your curriculum. They could serve as supplementary readings, catalysts for discussions, or prompts for writing assignments. You may also ask students to read these texts in book clubs and draw comparisons. See Figure 6.2 for more suggestions.

Leveraging AI for building text sets isn't just about saving time; it's also about broadening our curricular horizons. By turning to AI, you're able to access a wider range of voices and perspectives, while finding a balance between technological assistance and human insight. It's a process that involves experimentation and refinement as you adapt and personalize your approach to AI in ways that suit the unique needs of your classroom.

We encourage you to refine the AI prompt to suit your specific needs and teaching context. Perhaps you desire more contemporary voices or texts that specifically address technology and social control. Experiment with different prompts. And by all means, incorporate your own selections based on your knowledge of your students and curriculum. AI gives you a stronger start, but it is by no means the ending point of your instructional choices.

Whenever students are studying an all-class novel, it's important to also teach them how to *read around* the text by reading reviews, literary criticism, and related nonfiction. Experienced readers do this on the run, pausing occasionally as they read to deepen their understanding, especially if they are in a book club. Novice readers need us to introduce these habits and make it easy for them. A good text set alongside parallel stories, some reviews of *The Giver*, an interview with Lois Lowry, perhaps an article on dystopian literature and teens, and some articles on euthanasia will inculcate students into the art of reading around the text.

Figure 6.2
Practical Ways to Incorporate AI-Suggested Texts

Strategy	Description	Example
Bell ringer/do now	Read short poem or excerpts	Read Maya Angelou's "Still I Rise" before discussing resilience.
Thematic pairing	Compare themes across different genres	Pair *The Giver* with the nonfiction book *Quiet Power: The Secret Strengths of Introverted Kids* by Susan Cain to explore themes of individuality versus societal expectations.
Cross-curricular	Link literature with other subjects	Pair *The One and Only Ivan* by Katherine Applegate with science articles on animal habitats, adaptations, and ecosystems.
Multimedia extension	Pair texts with related videos or podcasts and other multimodal forms of expression	While reading *Hidden Figures* by Margot Lee Shetterly, visit nasa.gov and explore multimedia resources highlighting Katherine G. Johnson, Mary W. Jackson, and Dorothy Vaughan, alongside related STEM resources.

Ask your AI partner how the book you've centered in the curriculum was received when it was published. How was it reviewed? Was it banned? Was it embraced by particular groups? Then you can support your students with a starter text set that makes it easy for them to read around the text. Offering multiple related resources becomes especially important when you want to widen the perspectives and voices offered to students. For instance, you might create a Padlet so that as students read *To Kill a Mockingbird,* they can also read other authors who were writing about race and racism in the same era. They can read literary criticism, including by authors of color. They can access reviews. And they can read related nonfiction to better understand the context of the novel. Learning to read around a text lets you start your reading at a much higher level. AI can help you make it easier for your students to get in this habit.

For helpful text set resources and examples of Padlets that support whole-class novels, visit ai-enhancedliteracy.org.

Anticipating (and Minimizing) Hallucinations and Cultural Flattening

It would feel disingenuous to move into a discussion of nonfiction text sets without first addressing AI hallucinations, the term used to describe AI's confident presentation of incorrect information. Sometimes these hallucinations are easy to spot if you are already familiar with the topic. However, if you are unfamiliar with the topic, it can be highly deceiving when AI presents incorrect information as true.

Verifying the accuracy and trustworthiness of information is a critical skill in a world inundated with fake news and deepfakes. Kids are often savvy to the realities of fabricated information and already come to school with a robust digital media vocabulary. They understand terms like *clickbait, fact-checking,* and *going viral.* They can recall experiences with online echo chambers that present information based on their preferences and user history. Many can spot suspicious URLs, recognize sponsored content, and are wary of sensationalized headlines. Still, you need to weave these powerful lessons into your curriculum.

Every iteration of open AI is improving, because its training gets deeper. It is not likely, however, that hallucinations will ever completely disappear, in the same way that print media and publishing have always been plagued by inaccurate reporting, long before the internet. Part of reading is the ability to discern accurate information from inaccurate information. This will always be a critical part of classroom education.

One way we can begin to address this issue is by becoming more knowledgeable about AI hallucinations. If you understand the conditions that increase the likelihood of hallucinations and develop approaches to mitigate their negative impact in our classroom, you'll be better equipped to use AI technologies effectively. Also, remember that these technologies are ever-changing, so as the technology updates, you'll need to update your understanding, too.

Knowing when AI is most likely to hallucinate (see Figure 6.3) helps you stay extra alert and gives a clear picture of when AI is not the best tool to turn to for a particular task.

We find that AI consistently hallucinates when we ask it questions about topics we know are beyond the date of its most recent training update. It's easy to find out how recently AI has been trained. Remember, you can simply ask.

Building and Using Text Sets   137

Figure 6.3
A Few Times AI Hallucinates

- **Factual knowledge gaps:** When the AI is uncertain or lacks up-to-date information, it might fabricate facts, like providing inaccurate historical details, statistics, or references to nonexistent events or studies.
- **Current events:** If the AI is asked about very recent events, especially after its knowledge cutoff date, it may generate plausible but incorrect details.
- **Niche topics:** For subjects that are highly specialized or obscure, where the training data may be limited, the AI might invent terms, processes, or explanations.
- **Citations and references:** The AI can sometimes generate fabricated book titles, authors, or journal articles when asked to provide sources, particularly if the real information isn't readily available.

 What is your most recent training date?

 My most recent training data was collected up until October 2024. However, I can browse the web for current information if needed!

It is interesting here that the AI training date was several months before the time of this writing. If you ask AI for factual information past its most recent training update, there is a high probability that it will produce errors. For demonstration purposes, for instance, we can consistently get hallucinations if we ask it to tell us about a book published after its training date.

 what happens in the book brownstone by samuel teer

 "Brownstone" by Samuel Teer is a graphic novel that tells the story of a young girl named Brooklyn, who comes from a family of explorers and adventurers. Each generation of her family has a story to tell about their quests, involving magical creatures, hidden realms, and daring exploits. Brooklyn's own adventure begins when her father goes missing, leading her to embark on a journey to find him. Along the way, she encounters various challenges and makes new friends, exploring her family's legacy and discovering her own place in their history. The book blends fantasy elements with a narrative about family, heritage, and self-discovery.

 can you fact-check your response?

 Searched four sites

The book "Brownstone" by Samuel Teer is a graphic novel centered around a young girl named Almudena, who spends the summer with her father, Xavier, whom she has never met before. The story takes place in 1995, and explores themes of family, identity, and belonging as Almudena navigates her mixed heritage in her father's Latin American community in New York. The narrative delves into the challenges and growth that come from Almudena's new relationships and the cultural clash she experiences. The book also addresses LGBTQ+ representation and family dynamics in a thought-provoking way (Between the Shelves) (Forever YA).

For more details, you might want to check the book out on platforms like Goodreads or the publisher's website.

When we ask ChatGPT to tell us about a wonderful, recently published graphic novel, it fabricates a fantastical storyline. Ironically, it seems, we can easily correct this with a follow-up prompt: "Can you fact-check your response?"

Immediately, AI corrects all the inaccuracies and provides an accurate summary of the storyline by using a web search to retrieve the information. It goes to show that for the most up-to-date information, going directly to the source is the best option. Also, you can regularly ask AI to fact-check itself when you are dealing with dates, events, personal biographies, and other information that could potentially be wrongly reported.

While hallucinations are a concern, we tend to worry more about the more subtle ways that algorithms can culturally flatten, nudging us all in a single cultural direction by shaping our digital knowledge and what information is pushed forward for us to consume. Consider what happens when we ask for a list of middle school books versus when we specify that this is for a classroom.

List five middle school books

 Here are five popular books for middle school readers:

1. **"Wonder" by R. J. Palacio**
A story about August Pullman, a boy with a facial difference, and his journey navigating school life, kindness, and acceptance.
2. **"The Giver" by Lois Lowry**
A dystopian novel about a boy named Jonas who learns the dark truths about his seemingly perfect society.
3. **"The Outsiders" by S. E. Hinton**
A classic story about the rivalry between two teenage groups, the Greasers and the Socs, and the struggles of growing up in a divided world.
4. **"Ghost" by Jason Reynolds**
A powerful story about a boy named Ghost who finds an outlet in running, while grappling with a difficult past and striving to find his place on a track team.
5. **"Percy Jackson & the Olympians: The Lightning Thief" by Rick Riordan**
The beginning of a popular fantasy series where Percy discovers he's the son of a Greek god and embarks on a quest filled with adventure and mythology.

The books offer themes of friendship, self-discovery, and resilience that resonate well with middle school readers.

When we ask for a list of books without any other qualifiers, ChatGPT defaults to selecting books by popularity. These are great books. We also can't help thinking about all the other book titles we want students to have on their radar, illustrating what can happen if we do not take time to think about the behind-the-scenes inner workings of AI at the algorithmic level. When AI systems like ChatGPT generate lists or recommendations without specific qualifiers, they often default to the most popular or widely recognized options. Without interruption, either on the part of the AI developer or from us as prompters, dominant discourses continue to be amplified as they show up most prominently in the AI training data. When using AI, ask, why *this* information?

However, what if we change the prompt ever so slightly? When we ask for *books for a classroom*, we get a different set of books, ones that are noticeably more contemporary and very common in middle school classrooms.

 Can you list five middle school books for a classroom?

 Certainly! Here are five engaging and thought-provoking books suitable for a middle school classroom.

1. **"Front Desk" by Kelly Yang**
This novel follows Mia Tang, a young girl who manages a motel while her immigrant parents work tirelessly. It addresses themes of resilience, racism, and the immigrant experience, making it a great choice for class discussions.
2. **"The Crossover" by Kwame Alexander**
Written in verse, this book tells the story of twin brothers who share a love for basketball. It's a dynamic read that explores themes like family, identity, and the challenges of growing up.
3. **"New Kid" by Jerry Craft**
A graphic novel about Jordan Banks, a Black middle schooler navigating a new, predominantly white private school. It covers issues like race, identity, and fitting in, with a relatable narrative style for middle schoolers.
4. **"Fish in a Tree" by Lynda Mullaly Hunt**
This novel focuses on Ally, a girl who has been hiding her dyslexia and struggles with reading. The story explores the importance of understanding differences and the power of a supportive teacher.
5. **"Esperanza Rising" by Pam Muñoz Ryan**
A historical fiction novel about a young girl who must adjust to life as a migrant worker in the United States after leaving her privileged life in Mexico. It highlights themes like class, family, and perseverance.

These books are not only engaging reads but also offer rich opportunities for discussion, empathy-building, and critical thinking in a classroom setting.

Although we can try to guess why AI has made these selections, a helpful trick is to ask AI to explain its thinking. However, we must be cautious here and not assume that AI's explanation is genuinely a moment of self-awareness but more likely a post-hoc rationalization. Still, even when AI constructs a plausible-sounding narrative, it gives us valuable insight into the patterns and associations present in its training data. Asking AI to explain its thinking is a way to remind ourselves that each response we receive is based on an underlying set of biases that are built into the system and that there are many other possible responses than the ones that AI initially presents. We can keep modifying our prompts, pushing AI to draw from various categories of knowledge. The skill for us will be continuing to look for the gaps. "What am I not seeing?" That question can always be on our minds.

 Explain why these two lists are different. Explain your thinking.

 The two lists differ because they are tailored for different contexts and educational goals: one is a general list of middle school books, while the other is specifically curated for a classroom setting. Here's the reasoning behind the differences:

General Middle School Book List:

1. **Broader appeal and varied themes:** This list includes books like *Wonder* and *Percy Jackson & the Olympian,* which are popular choices among middle schoolers for their engaging narratives and relatable themes. The focus is on stories that might captivate a wide audience and are often read for enjoyment or as part of schoolwide reading programs.
2. **Classics and high-interest picks:** Books like *The Outsiders* are classics that resonate with adolescents' experiences of belonging and identity, while *The Lightning Thief* appeals to those interested in fantasy and mythology. These selections aim to hook students with stories that are widely beloved and known for sparking a love of reading.

By asking AI to explain its responses, we learn a little about how AI can reorder and recategorize information contextually. In the first list, AI prioritized popular titles, classics, and commercially successful genres. When we prompted AI the first time, we didn't indicate that these books would be used in a classroom. The explanation AI provides shows how the algorithm is aimed at reaching wide appeal. Choosing from some of the most widely read and enduring titles is a clear strategy for responding to our prompt.

It's so helpful to know that we can interrupt this pattern simply by providing more context in our prompt. When we ask for books "for a classroom," AI is able to reprioritize, arguably still aiming for wide appeal, but in a narrower and more nuanced context.

Books for a Classroom Setting:

1. **Diversity and representation:** This list emphasizes books like *Front Desk* and *New Kid*, which address diverse cultural experiences, including themes of immigration, race, and socioeconomic challenges. These choices aim to reflect the varied backgrounds of students in a classroom and foster discussions around identity, empathy, and understanding.
2. **Discussion and curriculum potential:** Books like *Fish in a Tree* and *The Crossover* offer opportunities for educators to connect the themes to lessons on character development, social-emotional learning, and inclusivity. For example, *Fish in a Tree* can facilitate conversations about learning differences, while *The Crossover* can be used to explore poetry and rhythm, making it an educational tool.
3. **Critical thinking and social awareness:** Titles like *Esperanza Rising* are chosen for their potential to introduce historical and cultural contexts, which are valuable for classroom discussions and projects. This aligns with the goal of helping students understand social issues and develop a deeper perspective on the world.

In summary, the general list focuses on books that students might independently enjoy, while the classroom list emphasizes diversity, curricular connections, and opportunities for deeper discussion. The selections for the classroom are intended to align with educational goals and help build a more inclusive, thoughtful reading environment.

AI cites diverse cultural experiences, connections to curriculum, and awareness of social issues as a basis for choosing award-winning books such as *Front Desk* by Kelly Yang and *New Kid* by Jerry Craft. This AI response illustrates how AI can work within a cultural context. Therefore, it always has the capacity to expand our knowledge across multiple contexts, but it can also flatten, or limit, our exposure, if we are not careful about what we prompt, how we prompt, and how we challenge AI responses.

Curating Text Sets on Nonfiction Topics

Creating text sets can be a time-consuming process, especially as the internet expands exponentially. We would love to have more hours in the day to sift through videos, articles, and other great texts, but the reality is, there are not enough hours in the day. It's much better to spend time curating from texts that are already vetted. You can use AI to curate and vet initial text sets that you can then curate further for your students.

Let's consider how to use edtech to rapidly analyze vast amounts of online content and identify high-quality, relevant materials that align with the curriculum.

Using edtech, it's possible to create multimodal text sets in minutes. For example, we can use Padlet, a digital canvas that allows users to collaborate and share text, images, videos, and other media. Padlet is an example of an edtech platform that has integrated AI into an already existing product.

When we ask Padlet's embedded AI feature to create a digital canvas to create a bilingual text set in English and Spanish about plastic pollution, it prompts us to give it specific information. The first textbox allows us to name our role. We are creating a text set for a 4th grade classroom. This context guides AI to pull more accessible texts, and it will be mindful of the age appropriateness of the content. Also, we'll specify that the text set includes videos, articles, and images. We'll want to give it some context by qualifying this information as building background knowledge and representing multiple perspectives on the topic.

> Generate a board for your class with the help of AI.
> I am a...
> 4th grade teacher
> I want to create...
> Create a text set of videos, articles, and images to help my students build background knowledge about plastic pollution. The text set should include information in both English and Spanish. The articles should be written at multiple levels of text complexity and represent multiple perspectives on the topic.

It takes about two minutes, and we already have a completed Padlet—a digital text set—organized into three columns: Videos, Articles, and Images. Each column has resources in English and Spanish. Visit ai-enhancedliteracy.org to access this and similar Padlets.

You can also prompt AI to organize the text set by subtopics, creating a natural learning progression from foundational concepts to more complex applications. For example, by adding "organize the information in subheadings," AI intuitively structures the resources to move from "What is the problem?" to "What is the impact?" to "What are the solutions?" while ensuring each section includes multimedia resources at different reading levels and in multiple languages.

AI enhances the way you prepare materials for your classrooms, especially in creating rich, multilingual research text sets. What would have previously taken hours of painstaking research and curation can be generated in minutes. Given the high demands and time constraints of this profession, creating comprehensible text sets so rapidly can feel liberating. It also opens up new possibilities for differentiation and inclusivity. By specifying parameters like grade level, language, and content type, you can quickly produce customized, accessible resources that support diverse learners and the multiple languages spoken in your classrooms. You can also swiftly generate text sets on various topics, allowing for more frequent updates to your curriculum that are responsive to student interests and current events.

Orienting Students to New Topics and Texts

The multimodal features of AI offer exciting possibilities for enriching students' pre-reading experiences. With AI's ability to generate and curate media—including images, audio, video, and interactive graphics—you can create immersive, multisensory introductions to new texts and topics.

This AI-assisted approach taps into the various ways students learn and process information, providing multiple entry points to complex narratives or unfamiliar contexts. As a result, students can develop a stronger foundation of understanding before they begin reading, setting the stage for increased comprehension and more meaningful engagement with the text. By offering different ways to explore a topic, students feel more prepared and confident, making it easier for them to dive deeper into the text.

Creating Visuals

Visual previews, in particular, can be powerful tools for orienting students to new texts, especially for emerging readers. By providing a visual representation of key elements—whether it's a story's setting, main characters, or central conflicts—these previews activate students' visual thinking and help them form a clear picture in their minds before they start reading.

AI can assist in rapidly generating or curating relevant images, timelines, or infographics tailored to specific texts, making it easier for you to consistently incorporate this effective pre-reading strategy. For instance, before students dive into a historical novel, an AI-generated visual timeline of key events can help them situate the story in its broader context, priming them for deeper engagement with the narrative.

Students reading *Indian No More* by Charlene Willing McManis with Traci Sorell, for example, would benefit from seeing the relocation of Regina Petit's family from their homelands in 1957 in the larger context of forced removal in the United States. That your AI partner can help create a visual timeline for *Indian No More* is particularly significant because it helps students grasp the long-standing impact of federal Indian policies on Native communities. AI can quickly generate a comprehensive timeline spanning from the Indian Removal Act of 1830 to the Western Oregon Indian Termination Act of 1954, situating Regina's story within a broader historical context of displacement and cultural erasure. This AI-assisted approach not only saves valuable preparation time but also ensures that students have a rich, visual understanding of the historical backdrop, fostering deeper empathy and critical engagement with the text's themes of identity, belonging, and resilience in the face of systemic racism and injustice.

In developing the notion of timelines and visual resources, we are deeply grateful to Rachel Talbert's work at Teachers College, which has illuminated the critical importance of centering Indigenous perspectives and scholarship when teaching about Native histories and experiences. This approach aligns with what Native scholar Leilani Sabzalian (2019) terms "Indigenous presence," which challenges the notion that Indigenous peoples and perspectives belong only to the past. As Gerald Vizenor (1999) reminds us, Native peoples are not merely historical subjects but active creators of their own futures, demonstrating what he calls *survivance*—an active sense of presence over absence, nihility, and victimry.

When creating resources about Native histories with AI assistance, educators should do the following:

- Prioritize Indigenous sources and perspectives.
- Challenge narratives that confine Native peoples to the past.
- Highlight ongoing Indigenous presence, resistance, and sovereignty.
- Include contemporary Native voices and experiences.
- Acknowledge the specific tribes and nations being discussed.

When you create visual resources about Native histories, whether with AI assistance or not, this understanding shapes not just what you include but also how you frame and present these narratives to your students.

Auditory Support

Audio texts, especially podcasts, offer a powerful way to orient students to new topics and texts. These auditory texts capture students' attention and provide rich context in an easily digestible format. Podcasts, with their engaging storytelling and expert insights, can introduce key concepts, historical backgrounds, or author perspectives before students dive into a text. Auditory previews not only build background knowledge but also support auditory learners and students who may struggle with traditional text-based introductions.

AI can create audio-based orientations to texts by curating relevant podcast episodes or even generating audio summaries tailored to specific texts. For example, before reading a novel set during the civil rights movement, students might listen to a brief AI-generated podcast that introduces and sets the historical stage, explains key terminology, and highlights central themes. This AI-assisted approach allows teachers to quickly create customized audio resources that perfectly align with their curriculum and students' needs, making the pre-reading experience more engaging and accessible for all learners.

Educators can input key information about a text or topic, and generative AI, such as Notebook LM, develops a podcast that introduces students to essential concepts, historical context, or literary themes, providing a valuable auditory component to pre-reading activities. Teachers can quickly create engaging podcast episodes that orient students to complex historical topics. For instance, to prepare students for reading *Indian No More*, upload a few reputable websites about the 1950–60s Indian Relocation program to the AI. In minutes, this information is synthesized into a concise, age-appropriate podcast episode that provides students with essential background knowledge about federal Indian policies, the cultural impact of forced relocation, and the broader context of Native American experiences during this period. By listening to this podcast before reading, students gain a richer understanding of the historical setting, allowing them to engage more deeply with Regina's story and the themes of cultural identity and resilience in the face of government-imposed changes.

It also sets up students with background knowledge to engage deeply with Native-hosted podcasts such as *Young & Indigenous, Native America Calling*, and *This Land*. Pairing AI-generated podcasts with human-produced podcasts opens avenues to expand critical media literacy skills. In our example, by comparing AI-generated content with Native-produced media, students can identify differences in perspective, depth, and cultural nuance, encouraging students to question sources, and recognize the importance of Own Voices narratives.

As AI technologies continue to evolve, you can use their power to create rich, multimodal pre-reading experiences. By tapping into AI's capabilities to generate visual aids, audio content, and customized resources, you can efficiently produce high-quality materials that orient students to new texts and topics.

This approach not only saves you valuable preparation time but also enhances student engagement and comprehension. By embracing these AI-assisted strategies, you set the stage for deeper learning experiences, allowing students to approach new texts with greater confidence and understanding.

Inviting Students to Co-Create Book Club Text Sets

Book clubs offer students choice, foster engagement, and create opportunities for rich discussion. When teachers enhance book clubs with carefully curated text sets, you deepen students' reading experiences and critical-thinking skills. AI is not only a powerful tool for teachers in this process but also a powerful tool for students who can work alongside their teachers, collaboratively creating dynamic, multifaceted text sets that enrich book club discussions and extend learning.

Traditionally, teachers have shouldered the responsibility of curating text sets for book clubs. Although this approach may feel like the best way to ensure high-quality selections, it can also be time-consuming and may not fully capture students' interests or perspectives, even when you've employed AI in your process. By involving students in the curation process and leveraging AI as a supportive tool, you teach valuable digital literacy skills and center students in the process.

To begin this process, start with a teacher-guided introduction for using AI responsibly to find supplementary texts. This involves modeling how to craft effective prompts and evaluate AI responses. For instance, if a group is reading *The Hate U Give* by Angie Thomas, demonstrate a prompt asking for related texts exploring themes of racial injustice, police brutality, and activism that center authors of color, ensuring diverse perspectives and voices are included.

From there, move into collaborative exploration with your students. Working together to refine AI-generated suggestions provides an excellent opportunity to teach critical-evaluation skills. Discuss which texts seem most relevant, interesting, or challenging, encouraging students to think deeply about thematic connections and consider multiple perspectives. This collaborative approach not only diversifies the range of perspectives but also teaches students to articulate the relevance and value of chosen texts.

Notice how a teacher guides a collaborative discussion, encouraging students to think critically about the AI-generated suggestions and their relevance to *The Hate U Give*, in Figure 6.4. By asking probing questions and validating student input, the teacher creates a collaborative environment where students actively participate in curating their learning materials.

In this example, the teacher is using the AI-generated list as a starting point for discussion, encouraging students to think critically about the suggestions, consider multiple perspectives, and actively participate in curating their learning materials. This collaborative approach helps students develop important skills in evaluating sources while also ensuring the final text set is diverse, relevant, and engaging for the class, all while deepening their understanding of the themes in *The Hate U Give*.

Figure 6.4
Book Club Transcript

Teacher (talking to book club): You've had some time to research the titles that AI recommended we pair with your chosen novel, *The Hate U Give* by Angie Thomas. Let's look at these together and decide which ones we think would be most valuable for deepening our understanding.

The teacher displays the AI-generated list:

1. *Dear Martin* by Nic Stone
2. *All American Boys* by Jason Reynolds and Brendan Kiely
3. *Between the World and Me* by Ta-Nehisi Coates
4. *The New Jim Crow* by Michelle Alexander
5. *Long Way Down* by Jason Reynolds
6. *Stamped: Racism, Antiracism, and You* by Jason Reynolds and Ibram X. Kendi
7. *I Am Alfonso Jones* by Tony Medina
8. *How It Went Down* by Kekla Magoon

Teacher: What do you think about this list? Which texts seem most interesting or relevant to our study of *The Hate U Give*? Are there any perspectives or themes you think are missing?

Student 1: I've heard of *Dear Martin*. It's also about a Black teenager dealing with police brutality, right? It might be good to compare it with *The Hate U Give*.

Student 2: I'm interested in *Between the World and Me*. It's nonfiction, so it could give us a different perspective on the same issues.

Student 3: These all seem to focus on the Black experience in America. Could we maybe look for something that explores similar themes in other communities?

Teacher: Great observations! Let's dig deeper. Why do you think the AI suggested *The New Jim Crow*? How might it connect to themes in *The Hate U Give*?

Student 4: I think it's because it talks about mass incarceration and how it affects Black communities. In *The Hate U Give*, Starr's dad was in prison, so it could help us understand that part of the story better.

Teacher: Excellent point. Now, let's think about balance. Are we covering different types of texts? Different perspectives? What might we be missing?

Student 5: Maybe we could ask the AI for some texts written by local authors or about experiences in our own city? It could help us connect the book to our community.

Teacher: That's an insightful suggestion. Let's do that and see what we get. We should also consider if we want to include any media beyond books—maybe documentaries, podcasts, or news articles about similar events to what happens in the novel.

As you engage in this process, you teach students about the importance of fact-checking and source evaluation. Students can learn to verify AI-suggested texts by checking publication dates and author credentials, confirming the existence of suggested articles or books, and cross-referencing information with reputable sources. These skills are crucial for digital literacy in an age of AI-generated content and misinformation.

 fact-check the list, are there any fake titles

 I apologize for any confusion. Let me fact-check the list for you:

1. *Dear Martin* by Nic Stone: This is a real book.
2. *All American Boys* by Jason Reynolds and Brendan Kiely: This is a real book.
3. *Between the World and Me* by Ta-Nehisi Coates: This is a real book.
4. *The New Jim Crow* by Michelle Alexander: This is a real book.
5. *Long Way Down* by Jason Reynolds: This is a real book.
6. *Stamped: Racism, Antiracism, and You* by Jason Reynolds and Ibram X. Kendi: This is a real book.
7. *I Am Alfonso Jones* by Tony Medina: This is a real book.
8. *How It Went Down* by Kekla Magoon: This is a real book.

All of the titles in this list are real books that exist and are relevant to the themes in *The Hate U Give*. There are no fake titles in this list. Each of these books deals with issues of racism, police brutality, or the Black experience in America, which aligns well with the themes in Angie Thomas's novel.

Encourage students to use AI to find or create multimodal texts to complement their reading. This might involve suggesting relevant podcasts or video essays, generating discussion questions for book club meetings, or creating infographics summarizing key statistics or timelines related to the book's themes.

After creating their text sets, it's important to guide students in reflecting on the process. Discussing how AI assisted their work and where human judgment was crucial helps students understand both the potential and limitations of AI in research and curation tasks. This meta-cognitive exercise deepens their understanding of digital literacy and critical thinking in the age of AI.

By involving students in AI-assisted curation of book club text sets, you create more engaging and personalized reading experiences and teach crucial skills for the digital age. Students learn to craft effective queries, evaluate sources, think critically about AI-generated content, and collaborate in a digital environment. Moreover, this approach empowers students as active participants in their learning, allowing them to shape their reading experience while developing important research and digital literacy skills.

The educator's role is to guide this process, helping students navigate the vast sea of information that AI can provide and ensuring that the final text sets are balanced, appropriate, and aligned with educational goals. You're not offloading your responsibilities onto students or AI but rather creating a collaborative process that teaches valuable skills.

This collaborative, AI-assisted approach to creating book club text sets represents a powerful integration of technology, student agency, and critical literacy skills. By embracing this approach, you prepare students not just for deeper engagement with literature, but for thoughtful, critical interaction with AI and information in their future academic and professional lives. See Figure 6.5 for a quick guide on co-curating text sets with AI.

Embracing Text Sets to Foster Choice, Student Agency, and Analysis

It takes more work to create a text set than to make a single text available to a class. It means the teacher has to do more work before class. You'll be rewarded, though, by classes in which students make meaningful choices about what they'll read, which means they'll show higher engagement. They are also set up to compare points of view, information, and craft across texts. Ultimately, you make it easier for students to be more analytical. It's always easier to compare texts than it is to analyze a single one. It's easier to see point of view when you have points of contrast. It's easier to notice craft when you read different authors on the same subject. We know that text sets are more inclusive because the multimodal aspect—the ability to include texts in different languages and at different levels of complexity—means more students have fuller access to the curriculum. But text sets also support your most powerful readers in being more critical.

Figure 6.5
Quick Guide: Co-Curating Text Sets with AI

Category	Component	Example Prompt
Essential prompt elements	Grade level and purpose	"7th grade book club exploring immigration themes"
	Desired formats	"Include articles, videos, and infographics."
	Language needs	"Available in English and Spanish"
	Specific perspectives	"Include immigrant authors and youth voices."
	Reading levels	"Texts ranging from 5th to 8th grade reading levels"
Information verification steps	Check publication dates are within AI's knowledge cutoff	"What is the publication date for each suggested text?"
	Verify sources and authors actually exist	"Please provide direct links or ISBN numbers for these sources."
	Cross-reference key facts across multiple sources	"What are your sources for these key statistics?"
	Ask AI to fact-check its own recommendations	"Can you verify the accuracy of these recommendations?"
Effective curation practices	Start with a strong anchor text	"Begin with *Front Desk* by Kelly Yang."
	Mix media types (text, audio, visual)	"Pair novel with NPR podcast episode."
	Include contemporary voices alongside historical ones	"Add current teen immigrant blogs."
	Ensure materials reflect student backgrounds	"Include stories from local community."
	Build in multiple entry points for diverse learners	"Offer graphic novel version option."

We are so passionate about text sets that every time we encounter a class where students are reading a single text, the first questions we ask are these: What might we pair with this? What pairings might let students see more or think more deeply? What perspectives or voices might I, and my students, have overlooked? And now you have an AI partner that can help you answer those questions and help you present texts in visually compelling ways.

Deepening Criticality with and Through AI

Teaching students to think critically with AI isn't just about learning to spot fake news or verify facts. It's about helping young people see how technology shapes their world and their opportunities within it. Researchers and educators like Henry Giroux (2022) and Paulo Freire (2021) remind us that education should empower students to question, challenge, and transform their world. Critical pedagogical lenses become even more important now as AI plays a significant role in creating the texts, information, and questions that students encounter every day. AI can help students become more critical—and they need to bring criticality to their interactions with AI. AI needs its users to be critical consumers, and it can deepen users' criticality.

Let's start with teaching students to be critical users of AI. Ezekiel Dixon-Román (2024) at Teachers College offers a crucial insight that reshapes how we think about AI-generated text: AI has no consciousness, no intent, and no real understanding. When you read an AI-generated text, you're not uncovering an author's message—you're "backward forming" meaning onto patterns that AI has assembled. This insight informs how you teach students to analyze AI-generated content.

Consider these critical questions you might teach students to ask:

- Who created this AI, and what data trained it?
- What assumptions might be embedded in its training data?

- Whose perspectives might be missing from its training data?
- How can we use AI to amplify marginalized voices while remaining aware of its limitations?

The questions remind both teachers and students that when AI writes, there's no conscious author, so you need to look at the system's origins in the place of the author's intent. Also, knowing that AI learns from existing texts, you must always be aware that it can reproduce societal biases. As this technology becomes more multimodal, so will the ways in which it carries—and in turn interrupts—these biases. Scholarship on multiliteracies, as discussed by the influential New London Group (in Reyes-Torres & Raga, 2020), demonstrates that meaning-making happens in many ways: through text, images, audio, and data. This multiplicity of channels shapes how biases can be transmitted and reinforced. When students learn to question not just what AI generates but why it might be generating information in a particular way, they develop stronger critical-thinking skills. Sometimes, as well, the texts that AI trained on were not acquired in clear, ethical ways. Rachel Talbert, for instance, warns how indigenous texts such as burial rites, which were not intended for public consumption, have been "scraped" by AI as it gathers its vast stores of knowledge (Talbert et al., 2024).

Critical lenses become especially important when considering how AI influences various student populations. Think about your multilingual learners and the tools they use. As AI becomes more prevalent in our classrooms, you must pay attention to how it supports students working across languages in particular. The goal is for AI to enhance students' ability to express themselves fully, drawing on all their linguistic and cultural resources. You'll want to set your students to studying, rather than accepting, AI-generated translations. They'll find that idioms are off and that usage isn't quite right in places. Often an AI-translated essay loses all of the student writer's voice and quirkiness. Your writers need to learn how to prompt AI to hold onto their voice and style, and they need to learn to reread what AI produces, thinking about how to retain their voice. This is exactly the kind of critical revision you want all your students to engage in: not just using AI tools but examining how these tools shape their opportunities for expression and learning. For instance, when students analyze how AI translates their writing and thoughts between languages, they learn to question what the translation says *and* how it changes their intended meaning and cultural context.

At the same time, AI offers the possibility of expanding your perspectives. It will make suggestions you had not thought of, it will give feedback you did not perceive, and it can be a creative, imaginative partner that extends your thinking. The goal isn't to make students fear AI but rather to help them approach it with both curiosity and careful questioning. We want them to understand AI's capabilities and its limitations, to recognize when it can enhance their learning and when they need to step back and think critically about its outputs. By developing this balanced perspective, students can learn to use AI thoughtfully as a tool for deeper understanding—of texts, of media, of their world, and of themselves. These are the kinds of questions that transform AI from just another classroom tool into a powerful lens for critical thinking and social awareness. They help students see technology not just as something they use, but as something they can shape and influence to create positive change.

In this chapter, we'll offer support with the following:

- Working with AI-generated texts.
- AI as a literary analysis and interpretation partner.
- Using AI to trouble nonfiction.
- Questioning, critiquing, revising, reflecting.

Working with AI-Generated Texts

When AI produces texts, especially from scratch, it will make assumptions about how that text should be organized. Prompts certainly steer the direction of its responses, and so if you prompt in critically minded ways, you'll get more critically minded answers. However, it is fascinating to see what AI defaults to when not given lots of context. For instance, we prompted AI with a very simple command: "Write a short text about a family dinner." We chose this prompt because it leaves a lot of room for AI to make assumptions regarding the context of a family meal. We were curious about how AI would ultimately come to a decision about who is part of a family, what sort of meal is served, the environment in which the meal is served, and the family dynamics surrounding this scene.

Deepening Criticality with and Through AI   157

 Here's a cozy scene of a family dinner:

The warmth from the oven had fogged up the kitchen windows, creating a snug barrier against the autumn evening outside. Mom was pulling her famous lasagna from the oven, its cheese bubbling golden-brown at the edges, while Dad finished tossing the salad with his secret vinaigrette. Sarah, the youngest, stood on her tiptoes arranging silverware with careful precision, determined to prove that at seven she could handle grown-up tasks. Her teenage brother Michael slouched in to set water glasses on the table, his typical adolescent attitude softening at the smell of garlic bread.

When they finally settled around the table, the chatter quieted briefly as Dad served the steaming portions. For a moment, there was just the clink of forks and the passing of bread, before the comfortable rhythm of a family conversation resumed, carrying them through another evening together.

We are fascinated about all the assumptions AI makes, from the autumn evening to the nuclear family arrangement—complete with Dad doing the serving—to the stereotypical male teen sullenness to the clinks of forks and passing of bread that exist alongside a sense of isolation.

But notice how these assumptions change if we prompt AI in Spanish.

 Escribe un texto brevo sobre una cena en familia.

Una cálida reunión familiar se desarrollaba alrededor de la mesa del comedor, donde el aroma de guiso de la abuela María impregnaba cada rincón. Los primos pequeños correteaban entre las sillas mientras los adultos compartían las anécdotas del día entre risas y el tintineo de los cubiertos. La tía Carmen había traído su famoso flan de postre, y todos esperaban ansiosos el momento de probarlo. Las conversaciones se entrelazaban como hilos de un tejido familiar, creando esa atmósfera única que solo

> se encuentran en las cenas donde el amor y la tradición se sirven en cada plato. El abuelo Francisco, desde la cabecera de la mesa, contemplaba con ojos brillantes a sus seres queridos, satisfecho de ver a toda la familiar reunida una vez más.
>
> English translation:
> A warm family gathering unfolded around the dining table, where the aroma of Grandma María's stew filled every corner. The little cousins ran between the chairs while the adults shared the day's stories, accompanied by laughter and the clinking of cutlery. Aunt Carmen had brought her famous flan for dessert, and everyone eagerly awaited the moment to taste it. The conversations intertwined like threads in a family tapestry, creating that unique atmosphere found only at dinners where love and tradition are served with every dish. Grandpa Francisco, from the head of the table, gazed at his loved ones with bright eyes, satisfied to see the whole family together once again.

It's fascinating to see how AI transforms its responses based on language. Once AI is prompted in Spanish, our family becomes Grandma María, Aunt Carmen who brings flan, and Grandpa Francisco sitting prominently at the head of the table. The sullen teen changes to little cousins. There is an emphasis on extended family over nuclear family, on real joy surrounding the sharing of food. The only change in our prompt is the language we use when interacting with AI—and clearly that matters a lot. Our linguistic choice shaped cultural references.

This is important information for educators to know, and it is wise to revisit the questions from the outset of this chapter—both for yourselves and for your students who are ready to deepen their AI literacy by beginning to understand and analyze the underpinnings of AI-generated passages. In "Artificial Intelligence and the Future of Teaching and Learning: Insights and Recommendations," Cardona and colleagues (2023) reiterate that "bias is intrinsic to how AI algorithms are developed using historical data, and it can be difficult to anticipate all impacts of biased data and algorithms during system design" (p. 8). AI is created with, by, and from human resources. It reflects human biases. Knowing that, you can also bring human critique to its education as well as your own. Zajko (2021), for instance, notes that just as AI can reproduce societal bias, it can also disrupt and counter them.

Visit ai-enhancedliteracy.org for some sample prompts that illuminate how AI may reiterate cultural references and stereotypes.

Let's return to our critical questions and apply them to the dinner passage:

- Who created this AI, and what data trained it?
- What assumptions might be embedded in its training data?
- Whose perspectives might be missing from its training data?
- How can we use AI to amplify marginalized voices while remaining aware of its limitations?

We recommend that you try this work with colleagues, sitting down with an AI-generated passage and working through each question. Developing an awareness of which AI you are using, whether ChatGPT, Claude, Gemini, CoPilot, Perplexity, or any other platform, builds an understanding that not all AI will respond similarly, and it highlights how little you often know about how AI was trained and on what data. These become areas of further research. On your initial go-round, try not to get caught up in all the things you don't know so that you can push to the questions about assumptions, missing perspectives, and amplifying marginalized voices, knowing that this might be tricky and potentially problematic territory for AI to reproduce.

Many of these questions can be tackled by studying AI's generated responses. You can look at who is centered in the text and who is missing. You can study how AI is reproducing ideals and stereotypes—the most common image of a Western family at dinner emerges as a nuclear family, or how when prompted in Spanish the ideal is a household filled with *abuelas, abuelos, tías,* and *primos pequeños.*

We are curious about AI's self-reflection when asked to analyze its response through these questions. It turns out, you can train AI to trouble its own work. We are also able to get some information about its training data. As we discussed in Chapter 6, it's important to remember that although AI can provide explanations about its training and reasoning, it's not "thinking" in any meaningful sense. We are observing outputs from a complex pattern-matching system rather than witnessing actual human-like reflection or comprehension. Nevertheless, these explanations can still provide valuable insights into how AI systems process and organize information, helping us identify potential biases, limitations, and assumptions embedded in their responses. Although

AI may not be truly thinking alongside us, it is certainly adept at mapping out connections and patterns that we can study and analyze for ourselves.

For instance, when we asked our AI partner to respond to these critical questions, it responds this way:

 Let me analyze the dinner scene text through these critical questions:

Who created this AI and what data trained it?

- I (Claude) was created by Anthropic, trained on large amounts of text data likely including literature, online content, and other written materials through April 2024. The cozy family dinner scene I generated clearly draws from common literary and cultural depictions of family life.

Assumptions embedded in the training data:
The text reveals several embedded assumptions about "typical" family life:
- Nuclear family structure with two parents, two children
- Traditional gender roles (mother cooking, father helping)
- Middle-class setting (having an oven, space for family dinner)
- Assumed family harmony and stability
- Access to fresh food and ability to prepare elaborate meals

Perspectives potentially missing:
- Single-parent families
- LGBTQ+ families
- Families experiencing food insecurity
- Different cultural traditions around meals
- Families living in small spaces without formal dining areas
- Families with different interpersonal dynamics or challenges
- Multigenerational households
- Families with different abilities/disabilities
- Working parents who can't prepare elaborate meals
- Different socioeconomic realities
- Various cultural food traditions

Using AI to amplify marginalized voices while acknowledging limitations:
- AI could be intentionally prompted to generate stories featuring diverse family structures, cultural traditions, and socioeconomic realities
- Writers from marginalized communities could use AI as a tool to help amplify their authentic voices and experiences
- AI could help translate and share family stories from different cultures
- However, it's crucial to remember that AI can only reflect and recombine what's in its training data
- AI should complement, not replace, authentic voices and experiences
- The best approach would be having diverse writers and creators use AI as a tool while maintaining their own voice and perspective
- We should actively question and challenge AI-generated content that reinforces limiting stereotypes or excludes diverse experiences

This analysis reminds us how important it is to critically examine AI-generated content and consider whose stories are being told—and whose are being left out. The seemingly simple family dinner scene actually carries many embedded assumptions that deserve examination and expansion.

Claude brings a lot of criticality to the text even if its default is to take up dominant narratives as a default setting when not critically prompted. What we learned from this experience is to be more specific in our prompting. If you want your AI partner to not center a nuclear family, you need to tell it that. Ask your AI partner to self-critique, which will help you revise your prompt design.

Bringing these questions to our Spanish version of this conversation reveals that the AI defaults to providing answers based on the language in discussion. Notice how Claude referred to Spanish written texts in providing its answer.

Claude's Response in Spanish (original)	English Translation
Analizaré estas importantes preguntas sobre el texto generado: 1. ¿Quién creó esta IA y con qué datos fue entrenada? • En este caso específico, yo (Claude) fui creado por Anthropic. Sin embargo, para ser transparente sobre el texto de la cena familiar, refleja principalmente patrones aprendidos de datos textuales en español, probablemente incluyendo literatura, blogs y otros contenidos culturales.	I will analyze these important questions about the generated text: 1. Who created this AI and what data trained it? • In this specific case, I (Claude) was created by Anthropic. However, to be transparent about the family dinner text, it primarily reflects patterns learned from Spanish-language textual data, likely including literature, blogs, and other cultural content.

2. ¿Qué suposiciones podrían estar presentes en los datos de entrenamiento?
• El texto refleja varios supuestos culturales específicos:
  – Una estructura familiar tradicional con abuelos, tíos, y primos
  – Roles de género tradicionales (la abuela y tía cocinando)
  – Una mesa grande con espacio para toda la familia
  – Recursos económicos suficientes para reunirse y compartir comida
  – Una dinámica familiar armoniosa y sin conflictos
  – La figura patriarcal del abuelo en la cabecera
	2. What assumptions might be embedded in the training data?
	• The text reflects several specific cultural assumptions:
	  – A traditional family structure with grandparents, aunts, and cousins
	  – Traditional gender roles (grandmother and aunt cooking)
	  – A large table with space for the whole family
	  – Sufficient economic resources to gather and share food
	  – A harmonious family dynamic without conflicts
	  – The patriarchal figure of the grandfather at the head of the table

3. ¿Qué perspectivas podrían faltar en los datos de entrenamiento? • Familias monoparentales o LGBTQ+ • Familias que no pueden reunirse por distancia o recursos • Dinámicas familiares complejas o conflictivas • Diferentes tradiciones culturales y étnicas • Personas que cenan solas • Familias que no siguen el modelo tradicional • Perspectivas sobre inseguridad alimentaria	3. Whose perspectives might be missing from the training data? • Single-parent or LGBTQ+ families • Families unable to gather due to distance or lack of resources • Families with complex or conflictive dynamics • Diverse cultural and ethnic traditions • People dining alone • Families that don't follow the traditional model • Perspectives on food insecurity

4. ¿Cómo podemos utilizar la IA para amplificar voces marginadas?
• Podríamos solicitar deliberadamente generar historias que:
  – Representen diversos tipos de familias y estructuras familiares
  – Incluyan diferentes tradiciones culturales y gastronómicas
  – Muestren realidades económicas variadas
  – Eviten estereotipos de género
  – Reconozcan las complejidades de las relaciones familiares
• Sin embargo, es crucial reconocer que la IA no puede sustituir las voces y experiencias reales de comunidades marginadas
• Lo ideal sería usar la IA como complemento para amplificar voces auténticas, no como sustituto
• Es importante que los usuarios sean conscientes de estos sesgos al interactuar con contenido generado por IA
 	
Este ejercicio de análisis crítico es valioso para comprender las limitaciones y sesgos inherentes en los sistemas de IA, y cómo podemos trabajar para hacer su uso más inclusivo y equitativo.
	4. How can we use AI to amplify marginalized voices?
	• We could intentionally request stories that:
	  – Represent diverse types of families and structures
	  – Include different cultural and culinary traditions
	  – Reflect varied economic realities
	  – Avoid gender stereotypes
	  – Acknowledge the complexities of family relationships
	• However, it is crucial to recognize that AI cannot replace the real voices and experiences of marginalized communities.
	• Ideally, AI should complement and amplify authentic voices, not substitute them.
	• It is important for users to be aware of these biases when interacting with AI-generated content.
	
	This exercise in critical analysis is valuable for understanding the limitations and biases inherent in AI systems and for working toward more inclusive and equitable use.

We realize, then, that we need to be attentive in our prompt design. We also realize that our linguistic choices will shape a vast array of cultural references. This means multilingual students may encounter significantly different cultural frameworks depending on which language they use with AI. Notice how our English prompt yielded a scene steeped in Western nuclear family traditions, while the Spanish prompt immediately transported us to an intergenerational Spanish-speaking family gathering, drawing from generalized Spanish and Latin American cultural traditions. These aren't just simple translations; they're complete shifts in cultural perspective.

For teachers, these realizations present both opportunities and challenges (see Figure 7.1). You can use these differences to spark rich discussions about cultural assumptions and representation, inviting students to compare AI's responses across languages and examine its embedded biases. But also be mindful of how these variations might affect equity and reinforce cultural stereotypes in your classroom. How might these cultural defaults influence your multilingual learners' experiences? By understanding these nuances, you can better support your students in navigating AI tools while developing their critical literacy skills. More important, you can help them recognize and question the cultural assumptions that emerge in AI-generated content, regardless of the language they're working in.

Figure 7.1
Questioning Linguistic Choices and Cultural References

Implications for Teachers	Opportunities for AI Critical Literacy	Increasing Equity
• AI will present different cultural defaults depending on the language used. • AI-generated passages provide an opportunity to explore cultural perspectives and challenge how AI reinforces stereotypes. • Multilingual students might receive different feedback or content depending on which language they use with AI. • Teachers can use these differences as teaching moments about cultural assumptions and representation.	• Students can compare AI responses across languages to identify cultural assumptions. • Classes can analyze how AI's default settings change with language. • Multilingual students can leverage their linguistic knowledge to examine AI's cultural biases. • These comparisons can lead to rich discussions about representation and cultural authenticity.	• AI may provide different quality or types of support depending on the language used. • Students working in different languages might get varying levels of assistance. • Schools need to be mindful of how AI tools might privilege certain cultural perspectives over others. • The variations in AI responses across languages could either amplify or help bridge educational equity gaps.

AI as a Literary Analysis and Interpretation Partner

AI can be a powerful tool for deepening textual analysis and interpretation. By prompting AI to analyze texts for bias, representation, and cultural sensitivity, you open up new avenues for students to engage critically with literature and media.

Deepening Criticality with and Through AI   165

Teaching students to interrogate texts before they read is a powerful critical-literacy skill. One way to scaffold this process is to have students turn to AI as a preliminary tool for research and literary analysis. Imagine teaching your students to research the literary context for a text by prompting AI with the following:

> I'm about to read [title of text]. What potential biases or perspectives should I be aware of as I read? How might this affect my interpretation of the text?

Let's try this with *The Catcher in the Rye* by J. D. Salinger.

> I'm about to read Catcher in the Rye. What potential biases or perspectives should I be aware of as I read?
>
> I'll help you approach Catcher in the Rye with an informed perspective. Here are some key lenses to consider:
> 1. Time Period Context
>   - Published in 1951, reflecting post-WWII America and its emerging youth culture
>   - Written during a time of increasing suburban conformity and materialism, which Holden strongly critiques
>   - Mental health was poorly understood and heavily stigmatized compared to today
> 2. Class and Privilege
>   - Holden comes from a wealthy, privileged background in New York City
>   - His criticism of "phonies" and society comes from a position of relative economic security
>   - His ability to wander New York, stay in hotels, etc. reflects his class status

> 3. Gender Perspectives
>   - Holden's view of women and girls can be quite problematic and objectifying
>   - His idealization of childhood innocence focuses particularly on protecting young girls
>   - His relationship with his sister Phoebe reveals a more complex view of female characters

In this snippet of a much longer AI response, we see that our AI partner alerts readers first to the time period that this book is written. AI points us to the post–World War II setting of the late 1940s and how this context shapes both the protagonist's worldview and the novel's treatment of issues like mental health, conformity, and adolescent alienation. This historical framing helps readers better understand the context of the novel and why certain attitudes and social structures appear in the text. For teachers, this creates an immediate opportunity to have students examine how the treatment of mental health has evolved since the 1940s. Students might investigate why Holden's obvious depression and anxiety are never named as such in the novel or why his previous "rest cure" is described so obliquely. They might research how mental health was discussed—or not discussed—in the post-war United States and compare that to contemporary conversations about adolescent mental health. This historical context also helps explain why Pencey Prep exists as such a bastion of privilege and conformity at this particular moment in U.S. history, when the pressure to appear "normal" and successful was perhaps at its peak.

It also helps readers to expect that although Holden critiques society, he does so while benefiting from significant privilege and status. This is a fairly complex point, and it's significant that AI can alert us to this point because it helps students recognize how Holden's social position as a wealthy, white, male student at an elite prep school influences his perspective. His criticisms of "phoniness" and adult society, although compelling, come from a place of considerable social and economic advantage—a nuance that younger readers might miss without this critical lens.

We admire some of the subtle moves that AI is making when discussing books from a critical perspective. We notice that AI does not misattribute the views of the main characters as simultaneously being the viewpoint that the author wants readers to take away. Instead, AI carefully distinguishes between Holden's perspective as an unreliable narrator and Salinger's broader literary intentions, helping students understand the crucial difference between a character's views and an author's message.

We are encouraged to see AI point out the problematic nature of Holden's view of women. From his infantilizing idealization of Jane Gallagher to his dismissive treatment of Sally Hayes, Holden's attitudes toward women reflect both his personal immaturity and the broader sexism of his era. This is precisely the kind of critical analysis that can help students examine character complexity without either completely condemning or excusing problematic behavior.

When we recently set students up to discuss their ideas about *The Catcher in the Rye* with an edtech AI partner (Flint) in preparation for book clubs, their AI partner significantly helped them develop their thinking. We taught students to share their thinking with their AI partner and then to ask their AI partners questions such as the following:

- Are there other parts of the text I should be thinking about?
- How does my idea intersect with other ideas about this part of the text?
- Are there angles or ideas I'm not thinking about that I should consider?

These 9th graders felt like their time with an AI partner led them to new thinking and to new parts of the text. It helped them critique their own thinking and bring deeper interpretation lenses to their book club discussions.

AI proves to be a powerful partner for literary interpretation—and you should approach it with the same critical stance you teach your students to bring to any text. AI's analysis of *The Catcher in the Rye* demonstrates both its strengths and limitations as an interpretive tool. On one hand, it efficiently surfaces important contextual information, identifies complex character dynamics, and raises critical questions about representation and privilege. However, we've noticed that AI sometimes defaults to commonly accepted interpretations rather than surfacing more contemporary or radical readings of texts. You have to prompt it to center feminist or queer readings, for instance. AI's interpretations are based on its training data, which may reflect certain cultural and academic biases.

We love AI as a thought partner as students rehearse their thinking as they prepare for discussion and develop ideas for essays. Students will also need to read articles and reviews, annotate their texts, and develop their thinking in anticipation of talking with AI and alongside it. For instance, you might have students compare AI's reading of Holden's character with their own analysis, asking them to consider these questions:

- What does AI notice that we missed?
- What do we see that AI overlooks?
- How might AI's training data or our prompt design influence its interpretation?
- How does our own positionality as contemporary readers affect our interpretation differently than AI's aggregated analysis of decades of literary criticism?

When we ask AI how awareness of these perspectives might affect interpretation, it provides a thoughtful framework that moves from surface-level character analysis to deeper thematic understanding. The response demonstrates how AI can help scaffold literary analysis in ways that gradually build student comprehension.

 How might this affect my interpretation of the text?

 Being aware of these perspectives and potential biases can significantly affect your interpretation of "The Catcher in the Rye" in several ways:

1. **Character Judgment:** You might find yourself alternating between sympathizing with Holden and recognizing his flaws. Understanding his unreliability as a narrator can help you critically evaluate his opinions about other characters and situations.
2. **Theme Analysis:** Recognizing Holden's biases can deepen your understanding of the novels' themes, such as alienation, loss of innocence, and the struggle between authenticity and "phoniness."
3. **Historical Context:** Awareness of the time period can help you avoid judging the characters or situations by contemporary standards. It allows you to appreciate the novel's cultural significance when it was published.

> 4. **Narrative Complexity:** Understanding that you're getting a limited perspective can encourage you to read between the lines and consider what might be happening beyond Holden's perception.
> 5. **Character Development:** Recognizing Holden's mental state and background can help you track his emotional journey and character arc throughout the novel.

What's particularly powerful about this response is how it builds from more accessible entry points (character judgment) toward increasingly sophisticated analytical moves (narrative complexity). Teachers might use these five lenses as discussion prompts throughout a reading rather than trying to tackle them all at once. For instance, starting with character judgments early in the novel creates a foundation for examining narrative complexity later. This scaffolded approach helps students develop their critical-reading skills gradually while maintaining engagement with the text.

Moreover, these interpretive lenses align beautifully with how students should approach any complex text—moving from initial reactions through historical context to deeper analysis of craft and meaning. The framework AI provides here could easily be adapted for other novels where unreliable narrators or limited perspectives play a crucial role, such as *The Great Gatsby* or *The Poet X*.

When we extend our question to include "And of the world?" AI deepens its analysis significantly, moving from purely literary interpretation to broader social implications. Notice how the response now helps readers examine not just the text itself but also how their understanding of the text might reshape their view of contemporary society:

> How might this affect my interpretation of the text? And of the world?

This is a fascinating question about how a text's biases can shape our understanding. Here's how being aware of these perspectives might influence your reading:

1. Reading the Text:
- You might notice how Holden's privileged background colors his ability to reject society's norms—his existential crisis is enabled by financial security
- You'll likely pick up on moments where his judgment seems particularly unreliable or shaped by his mental state
- You might find yourself simultaneously sympathizing with and criticizing Holden—feeling the universal aspects of his alienation while recognizing the limitations of his worldview

2. Understanding Character:
- Rather than simply accepting Holden's assessments of others as "phony," you might look deeper at why he makes these judgments
- You might notice how his trauma regarding Allie's death influences his interactions and his obsession with preserving innocence
- You could find yourself questioning whether some of the "phoniness" he sees is actually just adult complexity he's not yet equipped to understand

This response demonstrates how AI can help bridge the gap between textual analysis and real-world understanding. The first section about reading the text is particularly powerful in how it positions Holden's existential crisis within the context of privilege—a lens that helps students examine similar dynamics in their own world. When AI points out that Holden's ability to reject society's norms is "enabled by financial security," it opens up rich discussions about who gets to question authority, who gets labeled as troubled versus rebellious, and how economic privilege shapes personal freedom.

Similarly, AI's analysis of understanding character moves beyond simple character study to explore universal themes of trauma, judgment, and the complexity of adult life. Teachers might use these insights to help students explore contemporary issues: How do we judge others' authenticity in the age of social media? How do our own experiences and privileges shape our worldview? When do we, like Holden, mistake complexity for "phoniness"?

This kind of analysis helps students see literature not just as a historical artifact but as a lens for examining their own world and experiences. It's exactly the kind of critical thinking we hope to develop—where reading becomes a tool for understanding both text and society. See Figure 7.2.

Figure 7.2

AI as a Thought Partner for Literary Analysis and Interpretation

Step	Action
1. Start with context and potential bias	Ask AI to surface key contextual elements before diving into the text. This historical and literary context creates a foundation for understanding and some initial interpretation lenses while avoiding presentism.
2. Layer the questioning	Notice how our questions built from "What biases should I be aware of?" to "How might this affect my interpretation?" to "How might this affect my understanding of the world?" Gradually deepening critical questions helps students move from surface reading to critical analysis.
3. Use AI as a model for nuanced thinking	AI's ability to hold multiple perspectives simultaneously (like sympathizing with Holden while critiquing his privilege) provides a useful model for students learning to develop more complex literary analysis.
4. Connect to contemporary issues	Have students compare AI's analysis of historical texts with current social dynamics. For instance, how does Holden's privilege in the 1940s connect to conversations about privilege today?
5. Question the AI	Encourage students to examine AI's interpretations critically, asking what perspectives it might be missing or how its training data and our prompt design might influence its analysis. This meta-level of critique helps students develop their own analytical voice.

Using AI to Trouble Nonfiction

Nonfiction texts, particularly those simplified for young readers, can perpetuate problematic narratives and historical inaccuracies. When stories are condensed, nuance often disappears. Complex histories get flattened into simple narratives that tend to privilege dominant perspectives while marginalizing or erasing others. The deeper challenge is that these simplified texts often become the foundation of students' understanding about historical events, scientific discoveries, or cultural phenomena.

Consider, for instance, how many elementary school texts describe the "discovery" of America, or how science textbooks might present the history of medical advances without acknowledging unethical experimentation on marginalized populations. Well-intentioned attempts to make content age-appropriate can result in sanitized versions of history that dodge crucial conversations about power, privilege, and perspective.

AI can be a powerful partner in troubling these simplified narratives. It can quickly analyze texts for bias, flag potential inaccuracies, and suggest missing perspectives. When we show AI a nonfiction text and ask it to examine the piece critically, it can help us identify the following:

- Whose voices are centered and whose are missing.
- What assumptions or biases might be embedded in the narrative.
- Which parts of the story have been oversimplified or sanitized.
- Where cultural nuance has been flattened or erased.
- What cultural stereotypes are reiterated.
- How language choices might reinforce dominant narratives.

For example, let's look at this excerpt from *Missouri*, a 2019 children's nonfiction text by Jennifer Zeiger, which explores Missouri's early history. The text presents this information:

New Settlers

The first permanent European settlement in Missouri was Sainte-Genevieve in 1735. It was built near a lead mine. Then came St. Louis, which started as a trading post in 1764.

At the same time, Native Americans from Virginia, Georgia, and other southeastern U.S. states also moved into Missouri. They had been forced out of their homes by white American settlers taking over their land. White Americans came to Missouri, too. Some of them also brought slaves.

Textbox: Ships led by Rene-Robert Cavelier, sieur de La Salle, arrive in the Louisiana Territory. (Zeiger, 2019, p. 29)

One simple way to begin troubling nonfiction texts is to ask AI to fact-check. Although AI isn't infallible and shouldn't be your only source for verification, it can quickly identify potential inaccuracies and problematic conflations that deserve deeper investigation. This kind of rapid analysis helps teachers decide whether a text needs supplementation or replacement and what additional resources might be needed to present a more complete picture.

 Please fact-check this.

1. Sainte-Genevieve as first European settlement in 1735: Partially accurate. Ste. Genevieve is considered the first permanent European settlement in Missouri, but most historical sources date its founding to around 1750, not 1735.
2. St. Louis founded as trading post in 1764: Correct. St. Louis was indeed founded in 1764 by French fur traders.
3. Native Americans from southeastern states moving to Missouri: Accurate, but timeline is off. This migration occurred much later, primarily in early 19th century.
4. White settlers displacing Native Americans: Accurate, but again, the timeline implied is incorrect. This was a later process.
5. White Americans bringing slaves: Accurate, but occurred later than implied.
6. "At the same time" referring to American settlers in 1735/1764: Inaccurate. There were no "American" settlers at this time, as the United States didn't exist yet.
7. René-Robert Cavalier's expedition: While Cavalier did explore the region, this seems out of context with the rest of the information.

The text conflates events from different time periods, presenting them as if they occurred simultaneously when they actually spanned many decades. This oversimplification leads to historical inaccuracies, particularly regarding the timeline of European, American, and Native American movements in the region.

This fact-check reveals several critical issues that might not be immediately apparent to readers unfamiliar with Missouri history. Most significant, the text compresses events that occurred across many decades into what seems like a single time period, creating a misleading narrative about when and how different groups came to Missouri. The anachronistic reference to white Americans in a period before the United States existed shows how contemporary terminology can create historical inaccuracies—and how naming can act as a way of aggrandizing groups of people.

These kinds of fact-checks can serve as jumping-off points for deeper critical analysis. Once you've established what's factually problematic, you can begin asking more complex questions about representation, power, and perspective. For instance, how might this passage be rewritten to more accurately represent the timeline while also acknowledging the Indigenous peoples who lived in the region long before European settlement?

After identifying these factual issues and problematic narratives, work with AI to craft a more accurate and respectful text. Let's prompt AI to rewrite this passage, asking it to maintain grade-level accessibility while correcting the timeline and centering Indigenous perspectives. Here's what the AI partner suggests.

The Land and Its People

Long before European arrival, the land we now call Missouri was home to many indigenous peoples, including the Osage, Missouri, and Illiniwek Nations. These communities had developed sophisticated systems of agriculture, trade, and governance over thousands of years.

In 1750, French colonists established Sainte-Genevieve, the first permanent European settlement in the region. They chose this location because of its rich lead deposits and its position along river trading routes. Fourteen years later, in 1764, French fur traders founded St. Louis as a trading post.

The creation of these settlements began a long period of change for the region's indigenous peoples. Later, in the early 1800s, the U.S. government would force many Native American nations from the southeastern United States to relocate to Missouri and surrounding territories. This forced relocation, along with the arrival of white American settlers and enslaved African peoples, dramatically transformed the social and cultural landscape of Missouri.

Deepening Criticality with and Through AI

This revised text does a lot of important work. Notice how this revised version

- Acknowledges Indigenous presence and sophistication before European arrival.
- Names specific Native nations rather than using generic terms.
- Provides clear chronology instead of conflating events.
- Explicitly names forced relocation rather than using passive language.
- Maintains accessibility for young readers while being more historically accurate.

We can use AI not just to identify problems in our texts but also to help create more inclusive and accurate materials for our students, which they can either read or use as mentor texts for rewriting excerpts themselves. Although we should always verify AI-generated content, it can be a valuable partner in reimagining how we present history to young learners. The work we've just done with the Missouri text offers a replicable process for troubling and revising problematic nonfiction (see Figure 7.3 on p. 177).

Your AI partner can also help you review your library overall, simply by analyzing the titles and covers of books, for example. We asked Claude to look at the texts in a 7th grade classroom library, where students were about to research Indigenous peoples. We took pictures of the book covers and asked Claude about potentially damaging cultural stereotypes. Here's a sample response (visit ai-enhancedliteracy.org for the covers):

 The cover and title "If You Lived with the Iroquois" raises several concerns:

1. "Living with" framing suggests outsider perspective rather than authentic cultural representation
2. Art style uses stereotypical depictions with mohawk hairstyles and traditional dress in a simplified, potentially reductive way
3. Generic use of "Iroquois" rather than specific nation names (Mohawk, Oneida, Onondaga, Cayuga, Seneca, and Tuscarora)
4. Scene shows characters gesturing dramatically in ways that could reinforce "noble savage" tropes

This cover raises several concerns:

1. Use of "Amazing" in the title, "The Amazing Iroquois and the Invention of the Empire State" sensationalizes and potentially exoticizes the Haudenosaunee people
2. Again uses generic "Iroquois" rather than specific nation names
3. Historical engraving shows a colonial perspective, depicting George Washington meeting with Native leaders in a way that centers European figures
4. Subtitle linking them to "Empire State" could reinforce colonial narratives

For a 7th grade classroom, this book needs careful contextualization:

- Discuss whose perspective is centered in the narrative
- Examine how terms like "Amazing" and "Empire" frame Indigenous history
- Consider supplementing with resources that center Indigenous voices and perspectives

This cover raises several significant concerns:

1. "Legacy of the Iroquois: Traditions and Culture for Kids" uses dramatic, romanticized imagery that perpetuates stereotypes of Indigenous people as "warriors"
2. Shows a person in traditional dress against flames/embers, potentially reinforcing violent stereotypes
3. Again uses "Iroquois" rather than specific nation names
4. "Legacy" framing could suggest the culture is only historical rather than living and evolving.

The artistic style and dramatic imagery seem designed to appeal to children through sensationalism rather than authentic cultural representation. For a 7th grade classroom, this material would require careful discussion about stereotypes and representation in media.

Deepening Criticality with and Through AI   177

> Alternative resources by Native authors/educators would be more appropriate for teaching Haudenosaunee culture and traditions to students. Would you like me to suggest some?

Figure 7.3
Revising Problematic Nonfiction Texts with AI

Step	Action
1. Conduct initial fact-check	• Share the text with AI, and ask for a basic fact-check. • Look especially for chronological issues, anachronistic terms, and oversimplified relationships. • Note where the text conflates events from different time periods. • Pay attention to how AI flags both explicit errors and implicit biases.
2. Analyze language and perspective	• Examine how the text describes different groups of people. • Notice passive versus active voice (who is doing the action?). • Identify missing voices and perspectives. • Consider how word choices might reinforce dominant narratives. • Ask, "Who is centered in this story? Who is marginalized?"
3. Research deeper context	• Use AI to suggest what additional historical context might be needed. • Ask about specific Indigenous nations, cultural practices, and governance systems. • Investigate the broader historical context of events mentioned. • Remember that AI's suggestions should be verified with other sources.
4. Craft a more equitable narrative	• Begin with the peoples and stories that were previously marginalized. • Establish clear chronology to avoid conflating events. • Use specific names for peoples and nations rather than generic terms. • Replace passive language about displacement with clear descriptions of actions and responsibility. • Maintain grade-appropriate language while increasing accuracy and complexity.
5. Build in critical questions	• Create discussion prompts that encourage students to examine multiple perspectives. • Develop questions that help students connect historical events to present-day implications. • Include prompts that encourage students to identify what might still be missing.

With careful prompting, our AI partner destabilizes the colonialist leanings of this 7th grade library. It alerts us to cultural stereotypes, gives us language we can share with students, and provides a way to interrogate texts.

From here, we might turn to an AI partner to research names, including the names that groups of people call themselves and that others have historically called them—and the implications of those names in reflecting power and sometimes violence. We might research place names, as well as when and how they've changed. We might research cultural stereotypes that linger in popular culture and investigate their origins and legacy. Most important, our AI partner can continually alert readers to the non-neutrality of nonfiction texts.

Visit ai-enhancedliteracy.org for examples of AI analyzing potential cultural stereotypes in nonfiction texts.

Questioning, Critiquing, Revising, Reflecting

Your interactions with AI have the possibility of deepening your criticality. If you invite AI to challenge your thinking and your research, to raise questions about cultural stereotypes and missing perspectives, it will do so. If you prompt it to center historically marginalized voices and representations, it will strive to do so. If you ask it to critique its own production, it will describe its underpinnings and alert you to assumptions it is reinforcing. You won't ever know what it doesn't know, of course. It will know many things that you do not. And you will have knowledge it does not have. It's at this nexus of known and unknown that you can be continually questioning, critiquing, revising, and reflecting.

Conclusion

The future is already here—it's just not evenly distributed.
—William Gibson

Throughout this book, we've explored how AI can transform literacy instruction by expanding access, deepening criticality, and fostering more inclusive learning environments. We've seen how AI can help teachers create personalized decodable texts for readers who need phonics practice, translate communications with families, generate thoughtful feedback on student writing, and curate rich text sets that center diverse voices and perspectives. We've discovered how AI can function as a discussion partner, pushing students to consider new angles in their literary analysis and helping them rehearse their thinking before book club conversations. And we've learned how to train our AI partners to be more personalized, more culturally responsive, more alert to representation, and more focused on amplifying student voice rather than replacing it.

Embracing AI While Maintaining Humanity

The relationship between AI and literacy education isn't simple. Every tool that makes our work more efficient also requires careful consideration. When AI helps us translate student writing from Ukrainian or Mandarin, allowing us to fully grasp a student's competencies, we celebrate. When it generates feedback on student essays in seconds, highlighting beauties we might have missed, we're grateful. When it creates illustrated chapter books for older readers who need decoding practice or helps us find mentor texts that reflect our students' cultures and identities, we're excited by the possibilities.

Yet we've also seen throughout these chapters how AI needs human mediation. It needs educators to train it, to define parameters, and to ensure it doesn't homogenize student writing or flatten cultural perspectives. Most importantly, it needs teachers who understand that although AI is a powerful partner, it does not replace the human relationships at the heart of teaching or the striving that is at the heart of learning. When we use AI wisely, we free ourselves to have more of those irreplaceable human moments: conferring with writers about their progress, listening to readers describe their discoveries, and creating communities where every student feels seen and valued.

Moving Forward with Care and Innovation

As we look to the future of AI in literacy education, a few key principles emerge. These aren't rigid rules but rather guideposts for navigating this evolving landscape thoughtfully and ethically. They reflect what we've learned about making AI work in service of deeper learning and inclusive education. They remind us that AI is not an end in itself but a tool for achieving our most important educational goals: developing passionate readers and writers, fostering critical thinking, and creating more equitable learning environments. And perhaps most critically, these principles help us remember that how we implement AI today will shape educational possibilities for years to come.

Focus on Access and Equity

AI offers unprecedented opportunities to make curriculum more accessible and inclusive. Whether we're creating multilingual text sets, generating personalized reading materials, or using translation tools to deepen communication, AI can help us reach more students more effectively. We've seen throughout this book how AI can transform a teacher's ability to differentiate instruction, communicate across language barriers, and create materials that reflect students' cultures and identities.

However, we must be vigilant about how we implement these tools. New educational technologies often benefit already privileged communities first, while schools with fewer resources get left behind. The challenge will be ensuring that AI access doesn't become another marker of educational inequality. This means we must

- Advocate for equal access to high-quality AI tools across all schools.
- Support teachers in learning to use AI for differentiation and inclusion.
- Create policies that encourage rather than restrict multilingual learners' use of AI translation tools.
- Ensure that AI implementation enhances rather than replaces human relationships in education.
- Monitor how AI might unintentionally reproduce or increase existing educational inequities.

When we get this right, AI becomes a powerful force for educational equity, helping us create truly inclusive learning environments where every student can access rigorous curriculum while having their identity and voice affirmed.

Maintain Critical Awareness

Critical awareness becomes increasingly vital as AI embeds itself in our classrooms. We've seen throughout this book how AI can either reinforce dominant narratives or help surface marginalized voices, depending on how we prompt it and train it. The key is teaching students to question AI-generated content just as they would question any text: Whose perspective is centered here? Whose voices might be missing? What assumptions underlie these interpretations?

AI's limitations can become opportunities for deeper thinking. When AI provides oversimplified or culturally flattened responses, these become moments for investigation and discussion. Students can learn to ask why AI might have generated this response, what cultural stereotypes it might be drawing from, and what would make the response more nuanced or culturally responsive.

We need to help students understand when to trust AI and when to challenge it. This means verifying AI-generated information against other sources, noticing when AI might be hallucinating, recognizing when responses lack cultural nuance, and using AI as a thinking partner while maintaining their own critical stance. We want students to approach AI with discernment rather than distrust, understanding how to engage with it strategically and appreciating its capabilities while acknowledging its shortcomings.

Center Student Agency

The heart of literacy education lies in developing confident, independent learners who find joy and power in reading and writing. As we've explored AI's capabilities across these chapters, we've discovered that the most crucial work isn't in mastering the technology—it's in teaching students to make wise decisions about when and how to use it.

Consider the young writer deciding whether to seek AI feedback on their essay. They need to know how to prompt AI effectively and how to evaluate its suggestions, accepting some while rejecting others. They need to understand when AI might strengthen their work (perhaps in checking for coherence or suggesting transitions) and when it might diminish their growth (such as generating content that replaces their unique perspective or completing tasks that help students grow). They need to know how to learn from AI feedback so that they can apply it in situations where they won't access AI as they write.

These are sophisticated decisions that require both technical knowledge and self-awareness.

Our role as educators is to create environments where students can develop this discernment. We want them to practice using AI as one tool among many, to experience its benefits and recognize its limitations, and to make mistakes and learn from them in low-stakes situations. Also, we want our kids to develop confidence in their ability to learn with and without technological support. When students understand how to wield AI's capabilities while maintaining ownership of their learning, they become more powerful users of all available tools. This kind of thoughtful independence—knowing when to seek help and when to rely on one's own capabilities—will serve them well in a world where AI continues to evolve.

Embrace Ongoing Learning

If there's one certainty about AI in education, it's that tomorrow will bring new possibilities. Already since we began writing this book, AI's capabilities have expanded dramatically from more sophisticated translation tools to more nuanced writing feedback to more powerful ways of generating personalized texts for students. This rapid evolution can feel overwhelming, but it also offers continuous opportunities to reimagine what's possible in our classrooms.

The key is to approach this changing landscape with curiosity rather than anxiety. No educator needs to become an expert in every new AI tool or capability. Instead, we can learn alongside our colleagues and our students, sharing discoveries, questioning implications, celebrating successes, and working through challenges together. Sometimes our students will show us new ways to use these tools. Sometimes our mistakes will lead to unexpected insights. Always, we'll want to keep asking, How can this technology help us create more engaging, equitable, and meaningful learning experiences?

The future of AI in literacy education will be shaped by educators who maintain this spirit of curiosity while staying grounded in their deepest values about teaching and learning. We don't need to know everything; we just need to stay open to learning, keep experimenting thoughtfully, and remember that technology serves pedagogy, not the other way around.

Finding Joy in the Journey

There's something wonderful about teaching in this moment, when AI makes possible what we've long wished for: the abilities to differentiate extensively, provide immediate feedback, and make texts accessible across languages and reading levels. Yes, there are challenges. Yes, there will be mistakes. We will make mistakes, our students will make mistakes, and our AI partners will make mistakes. But there is also tremendous possibility.

We hope this book has given you practical tools for working with AI, theoretical frameworks for thinking about AI's role in literacy education, and most important, confidence in your ability to shape how AI is used in your classroom. Remember that you don't have to figure everything out at once. Start small with one area where AI might make your teaching more powerful or your students' learning more accessible. Share your discoveries with colleagues. Remain curious about what's possible while staying grounded in what matters most: developing passionate, thoughtful readers and writers who can use all the tools available to them, including AI, to engage deeply with texts and express themselves powerfully.

The future of literacy education will be shaped by how thoughtfully we incorporate AI into our practice now. Let's move forward with hope, wisdom, and an unwavering commitment to our students' growth as readers, writers, critical thinkers, and young humans.

Acknowledgments

This kind of study doesn't happen without many colleagues and teachers innovating and piloting in conditions of uncertainty. These are educators who are willing for things to be messy. If there is one thing we've learned from working with AI in so many classrooms, it's that when you work with an AI partner, it never does exactly what you want; it does something interesting.

We want to thank the schools, institutions, parent and educator groups, and teachers who have opened their classrooms and shared this work in process. Some invited us to pilot new work, some questioned us in ways that led to new terrain, and many shared what they were finding as they explored the complicated world of AI-enhanced literacy. In particular, we want to thank the following: PS 158 in New York City, especially its fearless leader Dina Ercolano and AI pioneer Alexa Hurwitz, who fostered an exploration of AI and personal decodables; the American School of Barcelona, especially their tech guru Ashley Holst, Head of School Mark Pingitore, Director of Curriculum Johanna Cena, Head of Upper School Omar Ugalde, and new-to-AI-convert Lauren Freer; as well as the entire 9th–10th grade World Studies team: Brennan English, Ted Pickett, Monica Francesca Villanueva, and Molly Brown; De Mots et des Crais, especially founder Yves Nadon and treasured colleague Diane Oullette; Rye City Schools, New York, especially Superintendent Eric Byrne and Assistant Superintendent Tricia Murray; all our colleagues at Teachers College, especially Rachel Talbert, Emily Butler Smith, Natalie Louis, and Coley Conter—whose generous feedback and friendship shaped early drafts. Special thanks to Francis Janosco and the teachers in Darien, Connecticut, who joined us on the cutting edge, exploring AI while so many were still hesitant. We're also grateful to the Buckley Country Day School community in Roslyn, New York—from the Head of School Jean-Marc Juhel, Lower School Head Elizabeth Lyons, and Upper School Head Dean Schlanger—to the innovative faculty who took an early interest in this work, especially Alana Gamber and Stefani Rosenthal, who were early adopters of these ideas and helped us explore AI's potential in real classrooms. Their willingness, along with so many others, to experiment, share their discoveries, and engage thoughtfully with new possibilities enriched our understanding of how AI can transform education.

We are grateful to ASCD for this opportunity and, most particularly, to our editor, Bill Varner, who believed in this project from the start and made it all possible. Thank you, Bill. Thank you as well to Liz Wegner, who took the manuscript and polished it up in magical ways. We so appreciate your expert care, Liz.

And finally, we thank our families.

From Mary: Thank you to Jackson Ehrenworth, for your many conversations about AI and for sharing your wisdom as we developed ours; to Rich Hallett, not only for talking over ideas but for making so many meals and sharing weekend time with a writer; and to my father, Paul Lohnes, who worked on the very first computers at MIT, and whose punch cards used to be our playthings.

From Phil: Thank you to Priscilla Seyfried, for the many date nights deferred while this book took shape. To my dad, Michael Seyfried, who said I should do something with computers—a prediction that finally came true in an unexpected way. To my mom, Eugenia Seyfried, who taught me to love reading and showed me the power of words. And in loving memory of Grandma Jean Virgina Seyfried, who didn't get to see this book come to fruition but whose influence lives on in its pages.

References

General

Allington, R. L., & McGill-Franzen, A. M. (2021). Reading volume and reading achievement: A review of recent research. *Reading Research Quarterly, 56*, S231–S238.

Baron, N. S. (2022). *How we read now: Strategic choices for print, screen, and audio*. Oxford University Press.

Bergen, E., Vasalampi, K., & Torppa, M. (2020). How are practice and performance related? Development of reading from age 5 to 15. *Reading Research Quarterly, 56*(3), 415–434. https://doi.org/10.1002/rrq.309

Berzak, Y., Katz, B., & Levy, R. (2018). Assessing language proficiency from eye movements in reading (arXiv:1804.07329). *arXiv*. https://doi.org/10.48550/arXiv.1804.07329

Briceño, E. (2023). *The performance paradox: Turning the power of mindset into action*. Ballantine.

Cardona, M. A., Rodríguez, R. J., & Ishmael, K. (2023). Artificial intelligence and the future of teaching and learning: Insights and recommendations. U.S. Department of Education. https://www.ed.gov/sites/ed/files/documents/ai-report/ai-report.pdf

Carr, N. (2011). *The shallows: What the internet is doing to our brains*. W.W. Norton.

Chakrabarti, M. (Host). (2018, August 21). The future of the reading brain in an increasingly digital world [Audio podcast episode]. *On Point*. https://www.wbur.org/onpoint/2018/08/21/reader-come-home-maryanne-wolf

Chavez, F. R. (2021). *The anti-racist writing workshop: Decolonizing the creative classroom*. Haymarket Books.

code-davinci-002. (2023). *I am code: An artificial intelligence speaks: Poems*. (B. Katz, J. Morgenthau, & S. Rich, Eds.). Little, Brown.

Cope, B., Kalantzis, M., & Searsmith, D. (2021). Artificial intelligence for education: Knowledge and its assessment in AI-enabled learning ecologies. *Educational Philosophy and Theory, 53*(12), 1229–1245. https://doi.org/10.1080/00131857.2020.1728732

Coventry, W. L., Farraway, S., Larsen, S. A., Enis, T. P., Forbes, A. Q., & Brown, S. L. (2023). Do student differences in reading enjoyment relate to achievement when using the random-intercept cross-lagged panel model across primary and secondary school? *PLOS One, 18*(6), e0285739. https://doi.org/10.1371/journal.pone.0285739

Cunningham, K. (with Burkins, J., & Yates, K.). (2023). *Shifting the balance, grades 3–5: Six ways to bring the science of reading into the upper elementary classroom*. Taylor & Francis.

Dewey, J. (1910). *How we think*. D.C. Heath.

Dixon-Román, E. (2024, February 13). Artificial intelligence is not immune to sociopolitical failures. Teachers College, Columbia University. https://www.tc.columbia.edu/articles/2024/february/artificial-intelligence-is-not-immune-to-sociopolitical-failures/

Dowhower, S. L. (1989). Repeated reading: Research into practice. *The Reading Teacher, 42*(7), 502–507.

Duke, N. K., & Cartwright, K. B. (2021). The science of reading progresses: Communicating advances beyond the simple view of reading. *Reading Research Quarterly, 56*(S1), S25–S44. https://doi.org/10.1002/rrq.411

Duke, N. K., & Pearson, P. D. (2009). Effective practices for developing reading comprehension. *Journal of Education, 189*(1–2), 107–122. https://doi.org/10.1177/0022057409189001-208

Dzotsi, E. (Host). (2024, May 31). That other guy (No. 832) [Audio podcast episode]. *This American Life*. https://www.thisamericanlife.org/832/that-other-guy

Ehrenworth, M. (2025). *Vocabulary connections: A structured approach to deepening students' academic and expressive language*. Routledge.

España, C., & Herrera, L. Y. (2020). *En comunidad: Lessons for centering the voices and experiences of bilingual Latinx students*. Heinemann.

Espinosa, C., & Ascenzi-Moreno, L. (2021). *Rooted in strength: Using translanguaging to grow multilingual readers and writers*. Scholastic.

Fisher, D., & Frey, N. (2021). *Better learning through structured teaching: A framework for the gradual release of responsibility* (3rd ed.). ASCD.

Freire, P. (2021). *Pedagogy of hope: Reliving pedagogy of the oppressed* (R. R. Barr, Trans.). Bloomsbury Academic. https://doi.org/10.5040/9781350190238

Fu, D. (1995). *My trouble is my English: Asian students and the American dream*. Boynton/Cook: Heinemann.

García, O., Johnson, S. I., & Seltzer, K. (2017). *The translanguaging classroom: Leveraging student bilingualism for learning*. Caslon.

García, O., & Kleifgen, J. A. (2020). Translanguaging and literacies. *Reading Research Quarterly, 55*(4), 553–571. https://doi.org/10.1002/rrq.286

Ghiso, M. P., & Campano, G. (2024). *Methods for community-based research: Advancing educational justice and epistemic rights*. Routledge.

Ghiso, M. P., Campano, G., Thakurta, A., & Ponce, O. V. (2024). Community-based research with immigrant families: Sustaining an intellectual commons of care, resistance, and solidarity in an urban intensive context. *Urban Education, 59*(2), 495–519.

Giroux, H. A. (2022). *Pedagogy of resistance: Against manufactured ignorance*. Bloomsbury Academic.

Grammarly. (2024, June 14). The future of writing: Creating the playbook for human-AI collaboration [Video]. YouTube. https://www.youtube.com/watch?v=J5e-clEnkws&t=1s

Hammond, Z. (2021). Liberatory education: Integrating the science of learning and culturally responsive practice. *American Educator, 45*(2), 4.

Hari, J. (2022). *Stolen focus: Why you can't pay attention—and how to think deeply again*. Crown.

Hattie, J. (2023). *Visible learning: The sequel: A synthesis of over 2,100 meta-analyses relating to achievement*. Routledge, Taylor & Francis.

Howard, J. R., Milner-McCall, T., & Howard, T. C. (2020). *Not this but that: No more teaching without positive relationships*. Heinemann.

Jabr, F. (2013, April 11). The reading brain in the digital age: The science of paper versus screens. *Scientific American*. https://www.scientificamerican.com/article/reading-paper-screens/

Jen, G. (2020). *The resisters*. Vintage.

Johnston, P. (2012). *Opening minds: Using language to change lives*. Stenhouse.

Kitroeff, N. (Host). (2025, February 25). She fell in love with ChatGPT. Like, actual love. With sex [Audio podcast episode]. *The Daily*. https://www.nytimes.com/2025/02/25/podcasts/the-daily/ai-chatgpt-boyfriend-relationship.html

Klein, E. (Host). (2022, November 22). This is your brain on "deep reading." It's pretty magnificent [Audio podcast episode]. *The Ezra Klein Show*. https://www.nytimes.com/2022/11/22/opinion/ezra-klein-podcast-maryanne-wolf.html

Lake, V. E., & Beisly, A. H. (2019). Translation apps: Increasing communication with dual language learners. *Early Childhood Education Journal, 47*(4), 489–496. https://doi.org/10.1007/s10643-019-00935-7

Lima Sanches, C., Augereau, O., & Kise, K. (2018). Estimation of reading subjective understanding based on eye gaze analysis. *PLOS One, 13*(10), e0206213. https://doi.org/10.1371/journal.pone.0206213

Mądrzak-Wecke, L. (2024, July 24). Humanizing AI is an ethical conundrum. But that doesn't mean we shouldn't do it. *The Drum*. https://www.thedrum.com/opinion/2024/07/24/humanizing-ai-ethical-conundrum-doesn-t-mean-we-shouldn-t-do-it

Mandouit, L., & Hattie, J. (2023). Revisiting "The power of feedback" from the perspective of the learner. *Learning and Instruction, 84*, 101718. https://doi.org/10.1016/j.learninstruc.2022.101718

Merod, A. (2024, September 18). Are schools communicating their AI policies to students well enough? *K–12 Dive*. https://www.k12dive.com/news/teen-ai-use-schools-policy/727327/

Mézière, D. C., Yu, L., Reichle, E. D., von der Malsburg, T., & McArthur, G. (2023). Using eye-tracking measures to predict reading comprehension. *Reading Research Quarterly, 58*(3), 425–449. https://doi.org/10.1002/rrq.498

Mollick, E. (2024). *Co-intelligence: Living and working with AI*. Portfolio/Penguin.

Mollick, E. (2025, January 26). Post-apocalyptic education: What comes after the homework apocalypse [Blog post]. *One useful thing*. https://www.oneusefulthing.org/p/post-apocalyptic-education

Mollick, E., & Mollick, L. (2023, September 23). AI as feedback generator: Harnessing the power of instant input. Harvard Business Publishing Education. https://hbsp.harvard.edu/inspiring-minds/ai-as-feedback-generator

Nagelhout, R. (2023, November 17). Better feedback with AI? Harvard Graduate School of Education. https://www.gse.harvard.edu/ideas/usable-knowledge/23/11/better-feedback-ai

Nash, B. L., Garcia, M., Hicks, T., Fassbender, W., Alvermann, D., Boutelier, S., McBride, C., McGrail, E., Moran, C., O'Byrne, I., Piotrowski, A., Rice, M., & Young, C. (2023). Artificial intelligence in English education: Challenges and opportunities for teachers and teacher educators. *English Education, 55*(3), 201–206.

Noguera, P. (2015). *City schools and the American dream: Reclaiming the promise of public education*. Teachers College Press.

Reyes-Torres, A., & Raga, M. P. (2020). A multimodal approach to foster the multiliteracies pedagogy in the teaching of EFL through picturebooks: *The Snow Lion. Atlantis, Journal of the Spanish Association for Anglo-American Studies*, 94–119. https://doi.org/10.28914/Atlantis-2020-42.1.06

Roberts, M. (2023, December 12). AI is forcing teachers to confront an existential question. *Washington Post*. https://www.washingtonpost.com/opinions/2023/12/12/ai-chatgpt-universities-learning/

Rosenblatt, L. M. (1982). The literary transaction: Evocation and response. *Theory into Practice, 21*(4), 268–277. https://doi.org/10.1080/00405848209543018

Sabzalian, L. (2019). *Indigenous children's survivance in public schools*. Routledge.

Sharma, P., Gero, S., Payne, R., Gruber, D. F., Rus, D., Torralba, A., & Andreas, J. (2024). Contextual and combinatorial structure in sperm whale vocalisations. *Nature Communications, 15*(1), 3617. https://doi.org/10.1038/s41467-024-47221-8

Talbert, R., Seyfried, P., Ehrenworth, M., & Todd, M. (2024, November 21). *Inviting learners to harness AI to disrupt colonialism and reclaim history: AI, social studies curriculum, and indigenous histories and futures* [Conference presentation]. National Council of Teachers of English, Boston.

Vizenor, G. (1999). *Manifest manners: Narratives on postindian survivance*. University of Nebraska Press.

Vogel, S., & García, O. (2017). Translanguaging. *Publications and Research*. https://academicworks.cuny.edu/gc_pubs/402

Warner, J. (2025). *More than words: How to think about writing in the age of AI*. Basic Books.

Wolf, M. (2018). *Reader, come home: The reading brain in a digital world*. Harper.

Zajko, M. (2021). Conservative AI and social inequality: Conceptualizing alternatives to bias through social theory. *AI & Society, 36*(3), 1047–1056. ProQuest Central. https://doi.org/10.1007/s00146-021-01153-9

Literary and Young Adult

Achebe, C. (1994). *Things fall apart*. Doubleday, Anchor Books.

Alexander, K. (2014). *The crossover*. Houghton Mifflin Harcourt.

Alexander, M. (2012). *The new Jim Crow: Mass incarceration in the age of colorblindness*. New Press.

Alvarez, J. (2001). *How Tía Lola came to visit stay*. Knopf Books for Young Readers.

Angelou, M. (1978). The mask. In *And still I rise* (p. 18). Random House.

Angelou, M. (1978). Still I rise. In *And still I rise* (p. 41). Random House.

Applegate, K. (2012). *The one and only Ivan*. HarperCollins.

Braxton, E. (2023). *Legacy of the Iroquois: Traditions and culture for kids*. Ethan Braxton Publishing.

Cain, S. (2016). *Quiet power: The secret strengths of introverted kids*. Dial Books.

Carle, E. (1969). *The very hungry caterpillar*. World Publishing.

Cisneros, S. (1991). *The house on Mango Street*. Vintage Books.

Coates, T. (2015). *Between the world and me*. One World.

Craft, J. (2019). *New kid*. HarperCollins.

de la Peña, M. (2015). *Last stop on Market Street*. G.P. Putnam's Sons Books for Young Readers.

Dixon, F. W. (1927–present). *The Hardy boys* [Book series]. Grosset & Dunlap.

Hinton, S. E. (1967). *The outsiders*. Viking Press.

Hughes, L. (1991). *Thank you, m'am*. Childs World.

Hunt, L. M. (2015). *Fish in a tree*. Nancy Paulsen Books.

Jen, G. (2020). *The resisters*. Knopf Doubleday.

Koonce, B. (Director). (2016). *Float* [Animated short film]. Pixar Animation Studios.

Kurlansky, M. (2011). *World without fish*. Workman.

Lee, H. (1960). *To kill a mockingbird*. J.B. Lippincott.

Levine, E. (1999). *If you lived with the Iroquois*. Scholastic.

Lewis, C. S. (1950–1956). *The chronicles of Narnia* [Book series]. Geoffrey Bles.
London, J. (1908). To build a fire. *The Century Magazine*.
Lowry, L. (1993). *The giver*. Houghton Mifflin.
Magoon, K. (2014). *How it went down*. Henry Holt.
McManis, C. W., & Sorell, T. (2019). *Indian no more*. Tu Books.
Medina, M. (2020). *Evelyn del Rey is moving away*. Candlewick.
Medina, T. (2017). *I am Alfonso Jones*. Tu Books.
Morrison, T. (1970). *The bluest eye*. Holt, Rinehart and Winston.
Munsch, R. N., & Martchenko, M. (1995). *The paper bag princess*. Annick.
NASA. (2017). *Welcome to NASA's modern figures* [Video]. https://www.youtube.com/watch?v=5E4Hy3PMizo
Native America Calling [Audio podcast]. (2021–present). Native Voice One. https://www.nativeamericacalling.com
Palacio, R. J. (2012). *Wonder*. Knopf.
Peete, H. R., Peete, R. E., & Peete, R. J. (2016). *Same but different: Teen life on the autism express*. Scholastic Press.
Quang, P. N. (2021). *My first day*. Make Me a World.
Quintero, I. (2019). *My Papi has a motorcycle*. Kokila.
Reynolds, J. (2016). *Ghost*. Atheneum Books for Young Readers.
Reynolds, J. (2017). *Long way down*. Atheneum.
Reynolds, J., & Kendi, I. X. (2020). *Stamped: Racism, antiracism, and you*. Little, Brown Books for Young Readers.
Reynolds, J., & Kiely, B. (2015). *All American boys*. Atheneum.
Riordan, R. (2005). *Percy Jackson & the Olympians: The lightning thief*. Disney Hyperion.
Ryan, P. M. (2000). *Esperanza rising*. Scholastic.
Salinger, J. D. (1951). *The catcher in the rye*. Little, Brown.
Sapphire. (1996). *Push*. Alfred A. Knopf.
Shetterly, M. L. (2016). *Hidden figures: The American dream and the untold story of the Black women mathematicians who helped win the space race*. Morrow.
Stone, N. (2017). *Dear Martin*. Crown Books for Young Readers.
Teer, S. (2016). *Brownstone*. Nobrow.
This Land [Audio podcast]. (2019–present). Crooked Media. https://crooked.com/podcast-series/this-land/
Thomas, A. (2017). *The hate u give*. Balzer + Bray.
Thomas, A. (2019). *On the come up*. Clarion.
Vonnegut, K. (1961). Harrison Bergeron. *The Magazine of Fantasy and Science Fiction*.
Wang, A. (2021). *Watercress*. Neal Porter Books.
Warga, J. (2019). *Other words for home*. Balzer + Bray.
White, E. B. (1952). *Charlotte's web*. Harper & Brothers.
Winters, J. (2023). *The amazing Iroquois and the invention of the Empire State*. Oxford University Press.
Woodson, J. (2018). *The day you begin*. Nancy Paulsen Books.
Woodson, J. (2018). *Harbor me*. Nancy Paulsen Books.
Yang, K. (2018). *Front desk*. Arthur A. Levine Books.
Young & Indigenous [Audio podcast]. (2020–present). Indigenous Youth Voices. https://settingsunproductions.org/young-and-indigenous-podcast-main
Zeiger, J. (2019). *Missouri*. Children's Press.

Index

The letter *f* following a page locator denotes a figure.

access
    as barrier and requirement for adoption of AI, 3–4
    future of AI and, 180–181
    text sets for, 131
accuracy, 9–10, 136
agency, 151–152, 181
AI (artificial intelligence)
    accuracy of, 9–10, 136
    benefits of, 133, 156
    coaching, 41, 43–45
    fact-checking, 138, 150
    goal of, 10
    humanity, maintaining while using, 179–180
    learning with vs. learning from, 50
    possibilities, 1–2, 17, 18–20*f*, 65
    training, 63–64, 69–77, 70*f*, 132, 155, 159
    training cutoff dates, 16–17, 136
AI (artificial intelligence), types of
    conversational, 15*f*
    general purpose, 27
    generative, 15*f*, 111
AI, barriers to and requirements for adoption of
    access, 3–4
    certainty vs. constant change, 13

AI, barriers to and requirements for adoption of—(*continued*)
    humanization, 8–10
    maintaining judgment, 9–10
    mistakes, 9–10
    professional development, 4, 5*f*
    staying current, 10–11
    teacher confidence, 4
    trust, 4–7, 33
AI, characteristics
    bias reproduction, 155, 158–159
    critical and creative, 67
    ethical, 155
    humanistic, 8–10, 66
    intent, lack of, 155
    intimacy created, 67
    kindness, 8, 9, 67
    self-critique, ability to, 161
    self-reflection, lack of, 159–160
all-class texts and responses, translating, 119–120

book club text sets, 148–151, 149*f*
boundaries
    collaborative, 32–35
    ethical, 32–35, 79
    maintaining in chats, 27

chats. *See also* edtech chats
    conversational memory in, 28
    deleting, 32
    focused on representative samples as student profiles, 31
    how AI reads, 28–29
    maintaining boundaries, 27
    multilingual, 120, 121–122
    with multiple student's work, 29–30
    protocols, 26–28
    saving, 32
    sharing, 32
    single student, 29
    when to begin new, 28
choice, engagement and, 131, 151
coaching
    AI, 41, 43–45
    students during AI interactions, 46, 47–48*f*, 48
cognates, learning in other languages, 122–124
collaborative boundaries, defining, 32–35
communication with students and families, planning, 82–83
communities of care and belonging, creating, 112–116, 113*f*
compound words, learning across languages, 124–125
content literacy, building, 130
conversational AI, 15*f*
critical awareness, importance of maintaining, 181
critical competencies, using translation tools for, 113*f*, 116–120
criticality
    developing, 131
    teaching, reasons for, 154–155
critical literacies, developing, 130, 165
critical thinking about AI, questions to ask, 154–155
cultural competence, teaching with, 129
cultural flattening, minimizing, 138–143

deep reading, 94–95
detection programs, 6–7
digital literacy skills, 148–151
digital reading. *See also* reading, the superpowers of
    advantages to, 90, 95–96, 98*f*
    challenges of, 90, 96–98, 98*f*

digital reading—(*continued*)
    comprehension, increasing, 98–99, 100*f*
    comprehension and, 95–98
    future of, 108–109
    multitasking while, 97
domain vocabulary, learning, 126

edtech, AI-powered. *See also* student-AI partnerships
    coaching students during interactions, 46, 47–48*f*, 48
    creating text sets, 143–144
    as a learning partner, 40–46, 40*f*, 46*f*
    tips for using, 58–59
edtech AI sites, 3–4
edtech chats. *See also* chats
    prompt design for, 27–28
    for readers below benchmark, 108, 109*f*
    setting up for student writers, 77–79
edtech tools, AI-powered, 16*f*
emotion, AI and, 8–10
engagement, choice and, 131, 151
equity, 6, 131, 180–181
ethical boundaries, defining, 32–35, 79
etymology, using AI to research, 126
exemplar essays, use of, 34
eye-gaze analysis, 93

fact-checking, 138, 150, 171–174
families
    sharing stories while translating to many languages, 114–116
    translating communications to, 116
feedback, 8–10, 60–66, 79
flow states, 94–95, 97–98
focus
    superpower of, 94–95
    when reading digital texts, 97–98

general purpose AI, 27
generative AI, 15*f*, 111

hallucinations, AI, 136–143, 137*f*
haptic dissonance, 98
human characteristic of AI, 8–10, 66

idioms, learning in other languages, 125
instructional planning, AI as a partner in lessons generated on teacher models, 22–23*f*

instructional planning, AI as a partner in—(*continued*)
    planning communication about writing skills with students and families, 82–83
    responsive instruction, 82*f*
    targeted small group instruction, 81–82
    whole-group lesson planning, 80–81

large language models (LLMs), 15*f*
learning alliances, 113*f*, 120–122
lessons, generating based on teacher models, 22–23*f*
linguistics
    competencies, deepening, 112–116
    hierarchies and inequities, dismantling, 111
    increasing teachers' knowledge of, 122–129
    teaching with flexibility, 129
literacy, potential of, 1
literacy education, principles of AI in
    access and equity focus, 180–181
    critical awareness, 181
    joy in the journey, 183
    ongoing learning, 182–183
    student agency, 182
literacy skills, digital, 148–151
literacy tool, expanding AI as a, 17–18, 18–20*f*, 20
literary analysis and interpretation, AI for, 164–171

models
    becoming conversant with, 14, 16–17
    large language (LLMs), 15*f*
morphology, using AI to research, 126–129
multilingual classrooms. *See also* translation tools, using AI-powered
    communities of care and belonging, creating, 112–116, 113*f*
    dual language stories in, 102–106
    transforming with AI, 111–112, 117
multilingual learners, translation tools for, 116–120

nonfiction texts, revising problematic, 171–178
novelty bias, 97

partnerships. *See also* student-AI partnerships
    instructional planning-AI, 80–83, 82*f*
peer discussion, fostering, 113*f*, 120–122
podcasts, 146–147
pre-reading experiences, creating, 147
previewing
    in digital texts, 96–97
    superpower of, 91–93
professional development, 4, 5*f*
prompt design, 21–24, 22–23*f*, 25–26*f*, 27–28
prompt language, examples of, 25*f*
prompts
    ethical vs. unethical, 34, 35*f*
    examples of revising, 139–142
    responses and assumptions with, 156–164
    strategies, effective, 25–26*f*
    training for, 6–7, 21
punishment for using AI, inequity in, 6
purpose, choosing AI environments matched to, 20–21

readers below benchmark, supporting with
    creating personal decodable texts, 101–102
    dual language stories, 102–106
    edtech chat rooms, 108, 109*f*
    illustrated stories, 106–108
reading, the superpowers of. *See also* digital reading
    focus, 94–95
    previewing, 91–93, 96–97
    rereading, 93–94, 97
reading comprehension, 90, 93–99, 100*f*, 130
rereading
    in digital texts, 97
    superpower of, 93–94

search engines vs. AI tools, 16
skills, transferable, 14
small group instruction, targeted, 81–82
storytelling, sharing while translating to many languages, 114–116
student-AI partnerships
    to challenge, 54
    coaching during AI interactions, 46, 47–48*f*, 48

student-AI partnerships—(*continued*)
    to increase access, 51*f*
    to increase complexity of learning, 50–55, 51*f*
    setting up AI as a learning partner, 40–46, 40*f*, 46*f*
    to support skill progression, 55*f*
    to support with growth and independence, 48–55, 55*f*
    unexpected interactions, embracing, 55–58
student writers
    coaching alongside AI, 83–84, 85*f*
    setting up edtech chats for, 77–79
    sharing stories while translating to many languages, 114–116
    sharing your process and AI interactions with, 85–88
    translating the writing of, 118–120

teachers
    linguistics knowledge, increasing, 122–129
    requirement for AI adoption, 4
terminology, becoming conversant with, 14, 15–16*f*, 17
texts, critical thinking about AI-generated
    cultural references, 161–164, 164*f*
    linguistic choices, 162–164, 164*f*
    for literary analysis and interpretation, 164–171
    nonfiction, 171–178
    responses and assumptions with, 156–164
text sets
    book club, student creation of, 148–151, 149*f*
    co-curating, 152*f*
    creating for a whole-class novel, 131–135, 133*f*, 135*f*
    cultural flattening, minimizing, 138–143
    to foster choice, 151–153
    hallucinations, anticipating, 136–138, 137*f*
    multilingual, 119
    nonfiction topics, 143–144
    orienting with visual and audio-based, 145–147

text sets—(*continued*)
    purpose of, 130–131
    for student agency, 151–152
thinking, reflective, 12
tools
    edtech, AI-powered, 16*f*
    search engines vs. AI, 16
training AI, 63–64, 69–77, 70*f*, 132, 155, 159
training cutoff dates, AI, 16–17, 136
translanguaging, 116–120
translations, AI-generated, 155
translation tools, using AI-powered
    to create multilingual text sets, 119
    creating communities of care and belonging, 112–116, 113*f*
    to foster peer discussion, 113*f*, 120–122
    to grasp and deepen students' critical competencies, 113*f*, 116–120
    increasing teachers' knowledge of linguistics, 122–129
    for learning alliances, 113*f*, 120–122
    for multilingual learners, 116–120
    to translate all-class texts and responses, 119–120
trust
    cultivating a culture of, 33
    requirement for AI adoption, 4–7

whole-class
    novel instruction, text sets for, 131–135, 133*f*, 135*f*
    texts and responses, translating, 119–120
whole-group lesson planning, 80–81
writing coach, AI as a
    across the writing process, 66–69, 67–68*f*
    coaching student writers alongside, 83–84, 85*f*
    edtech chats, 77–79
    for feedback, 60–61
    setting ethical boundaries, 79
    setting support boundaries, 79
    training, 69–77
    what AI sees in student writing, 61–65
writing feedback, 60–66, 79

About the Authors

**Mary Ehrenworth,** EdD, co-led a think tank on global literacy at Teachers College, Columbia University, for 20 years. She now runs Ehrenworth Literacy Innovations, working nationally and globally to empower teachers and students through critical literacies and collaborative inquiry. Mary's degrees include a BA in history and literature from Harvard and an MA and EdD in curriculum and teaching from Columbia University. Her most recent research fields are AI and literacy, and vocabulary acquisition. From that day long ago when a beloved teacher gave her *The Secret Garden*, to the days she now spends supporting children and teachers in becoming powerful and passionate readers and writers, Mary has been lucky enough to spend her time among things she loves best: books, kids, and teachers.

**Philip Seyfried** is a doctoral student in curriculum and teaching at Teachers College, Columbia University, focusing his research on the intersection of digital literacy and artificial intelligence in education. With over a decade of experience as a middle school language arts and literature teacher, Philip now supports schools and edtech companies as a literacy and digital literacy consultant. Currently, he's exploring how AI tools can benefit diverse learners and build stronger critical-thinking skills. Whether consulting on literacy practices or leading professional development, Philip champions approaches that welcome innovation while valuing what matters most—the human connections that make learning meaningful.

Related ASCD Resources

At the time of publication, the following resources were available (ASCD stock numbers in parentheses).

The AI Assist: Strategies for Integrating AI into the Very Human Act of Teaching by Nathan Lang-Raad (#124030)

AI with Intention: Principles and Action Steps for Teachers and School Leaders by Tony Frontier (#124032)

Applying the Science of Reading (Quick Reference Guide) by Mark Weakland (#QRG124029)

Beyond the Science of Reading: Connecting Literacy Instruction to the Science of Learning by Natalie Wexler (#125006)

EdTech Essentials: 12 Strategies for Every Classroom in the Age of AI, 2nd Edition, by Monica Burns (#124028)

Prompting Deeper Discussions: A Teacher's Guide to Crafting Great Questions by Matthew R. Kay (#124031)

Using AI Chatbots to Enhance Planning and Instruction (Quick Reference Guide) by Monica Burns (#QRG123066)

Using Technology in a Differentiated Classroom: Strategies and Tools for Designing Engaging, Effective, Efficient & Equitable Learning by Clare R. Kilbane and Natalie B. Milman (#120002)

For up-to-date information about ASCD resources, go to **www.ascd.org.** You can search the complete archives of *Educational Leadership* at **www.ascd.org/el.** To contact us, send an email to member@ascd.org or call 1-800-933-2723 or 703-578-9600.

DON'T MISS A SINGLE ISSUE OF THIS AWARD-WINNING MAGAZINE.

iste+ascd
educational leadership

If you belong to a Professional Learning Community, you may be looking for a way to get your fellow educators' minds around a complex topic. Why not delve into a relevant theme issue of *Educational Leadership*, the journal written by educators for educators?

Subscribe now and browse or purchase back issues of our flagship publication at **www.ascd.org/el**. Discounts on bulk purchases are available.

iste+ascd

Arlington, VA USA
1-800-933-2723

www.ascd.org
www.iste.org

www.ingramcontent.com/pod-product-compliance
Lightning Source LLC
Chambersburg PA
CBHW060538010526
44119CB00052B/748